SIX AGAINST CRIME

Treasury Agencies in Action

The real story of the U. S. Treasury law-enforcement
agencies in action, told by a man who for 31 years
was a member of the U. S. Secret Service and Assistant
Chief on his retirement in 1957. The Secret Service,
which protects the President and Vice President and
suppresses counterfeiting and check forgery, is only
one of the Treasury Enforcement Agencies. The
others are the Bureau of Narcotics which fights dope
dealers and the drug evil; the Bureau of Customs
which combats smugglers; the Alcohol and Tobacco
Tax Division, nemesis of the moonshiner, bootlegger
and gangland gunslinger; the Intelligence Division
whose agents track down the tax cheats; and the
U. S. Coast Guard which works closely with the others
to spike smuggling, rum-running and illicit drug
rackets. Here are exciting, true stories that reveal the
ingenious methods, the efficiency and bravery of the
Treasury detectives in coping with the cunning of law
evaders. The author also gives a history of the Treasury Department and includes valuable information on
how to become a Treasury Agent.

Books by Harry Edward Neal

INFORMATIONAL

COMMUNICATION
From Stone Age to Space Age

DIARY OF DEMOCRACY
The Story of Political Parties in America

FROM SPINNING WHEEL TO SPACECRAFT
The Story of the Industrial Revolution

THE MYSTERY OF TIME

SIX AGAINST CRIME
Treasury Agencies in Action

THE TELESCOPE

TREASURES BY THE MILLIONS
The Story of the Smithsonian Institution

CAREER

DISEASE DETECTIVES
Your Career in Medical Research

ENGINEERS UNLIMITED
Your Career in Engineering

MONEY MASTERS
Your Career in Banking

NATURE'S GUARDIANS
Your Career in Conservation

PATHFINDERS U.S.A.
Your Career on Land, Sea and Air

SKYBLAZERS
Your Career in Aviation

YOUR CAREER IN ELECTRONICS

YOUR CAREER IN FOREIGN SERVICE

SIX AGAINST CRIME

Treasury Agencies in Action

BY
HARRY
EDWARD
NEAL

Illustrated with photographs

JULIAN MESSNER   New York

Published simultaneously in the United States and Canada by
Julian Messner, a division of Simon & Schuster, Inc.,
1 West 39 Street, New York, N.Y. 10018. All rights reserved.

Sixth Printing, 1967

We are grateful to the following for the
use of their photographs: the Treasury
Department, U. S. Public Health Service,
Pan American World Airways System.

Printed in the United States of America
Library of Congress Catalog Card No. 59-7017

INTRODUCTION

In 1957 I retired as Assistant Chief of the United States Secret Service, a Treasury Department law-enforcement agency for which I began work as a stenographer in 1926.

During my Secret Service career I was frequently introduced by unwitting acquaintances to their friends with a brief biographical note such as, "Mr. Neal is an FBI man."

Whenever that happened, I made it a point to correct the speaker and to explain that the Secret Service had no connection whatever with the Federal Bureau of Investigation, an agency of the Department of Justice. No Secret Service agent wants to be identified as an FBI man.

The reason why a great many Americans (including some newspapers) associate all Federal law enforcement with the FBI is that the FBI has been more widely publicized, glamorized, idealized and advertised than any other government crime-fighting bureau. This is not intended as a criticism. It is more like sour grapes, because I am only sorry that the Secret Service publicity policy—long before the FBI was born—was to work quietly and without fanfare. Even now it does not go publicity mad. Had it blown its own horn and headlined the many accomplishments of its earlier years with showmanship and razzle-dazzle, the Secret Service might today be on the Glory Road with all the men, money and equipment that it really needs to continue its never-ending war on a thriving and modern underworld.

I have mentioned the Secret Service particularly because I was a part of it for so many years. Actually, though, the Secret Service is only one in a "family" of law-enforcement brothers comprising the Treasury law-enforcement agencies, and my task is to tell you, the reader, about these law men and their battles against the criminals who prey upon all law-abiding citizens.

In doing this I have chosen to disguise the real names of Treasury agents and criminals alike, except in a few instances where it is obvious or explained in the text that the true names are used. I have also used the true names of agency heads and supervisors.

The stories about the work done by the agents are, I believe, unusual in one important respect. The facts are not distorted in any way. Perhaps you have seen movies or television programs, or heard radio broadcasts, or have read magazine articles or books about Treasury agents, in which the statement is made: "This story is *based* upon an actual Treasury Department case." In some of the Secret Service stories I have seen or read which were "based upon" real cases, the base was so far away that the agents who developed the real investigations had difficulty in identifying their experiences.

I have therefore attempted to show how the average Treasury agent develops a typical case, for it is his day-to-day work that helps to clamp the lid on crime. Gunfire and guts are not as frequently needed—or used—as are brains and just plain luck in any phase of law enforcement.

Mr. Myles J. Ambrose, Assistant to the Secretary for Law Enforcement, cleared the path for me at Treasury headquarters to get material from all of the agencies, and arranged to have my manuscript reviewed for factual accuracy.

With the way paved, I then talked with many good friends and former associates at the Treasury in Washington. First and foremost was U. E. Baughman, Chief of the Secret Service, with whom I served at the time of my retirement as his assistant. Here I also had enjoyable and productive visits with my friends and one-time colleagues Deputy Chief Russell (Buck) Daniel, Assistant Chief (Security) Edgar A. Wildy, and Chief Inspector Michael W. Torina (with whom I worked in New York City years ago). These, incidentally, are all career Secret Service men with long experience in the field.

Mr. Harry Anslinger, Commissioner of Narcotics, and my friend, the late George Cunningham, Deputy Commissioner, welcomed my project and furnished the interesting case material about the Bureau of Narcotics and the illicit drug traffic.

Before visiting the offices of the Alcohol and Tobacco Tax Division and the Intelligence Division, I called on my good friend Henry Schneider, Deputy Director of Information for the Internal Revenue Service, who made the necessary appointments for me and accompanied me to the headquarters of these two branches. Henry was also very helpful in providing information about moonshiners and tax cheats.

In the Alcohol and Tobacco Tax Division, Mr. Thomas Bailey, Chief of the Enforcement Branch, talked generally about the problem of illicit liquor distilleries, then turned me over to Mr. Harry Lieberman, a member of his staff, who dug out closed case files and helped me to get down to the facts I needed to tell the ATTD story.

Mr. Perry August, Chief of the Intelligence Division, received me most graciously, and after briefing me upon the current activities of his unit he referred me to Mr. Gilbert Haley, Assistant Chief of the Co-ordination Section, who was most helpful in selecting much of the material I have used to describe the fight against tax cheats and frauds.

I obtained considerable helpful information about the Intelligence Division and the ATTD from my good friend

George Coffelt of the Internal Revenue Information Service, with whom I had frequently worked on other projects when he and I were both stationed in the Treasury Building.

And I must not forget to give credit to Bob Dillon, another friend in the Treasury Information Service, for it was Bob with whom I originally discussed plans for this book, and who, with Leon Siler (now retired), encouraged me to write it.

In the Bureau of Customs my friend Deputy Commissioner Chester A. Emerick and his associates Assistant Deputy Commissioners Frank Russell and Irving S. Brown, with the approval of Commissioner Ralph Kelly, gave me a short course in Customs work and provided the information which enabled me to set out the facts in smuggling cases as they are developed in the daily routine of Customs agents and inspectors. And I would certainly be ungrateful if I did not include my thanks to Mr. Emerick's efficient secretary Mrs. Sally E. Miller, who, like all good secretaries, knows how and where to find answers to difficult questions.

My Coast Guard "guide" was Information Specialist H. R. Kaplan, who strongly recommended that I tell the story about the CG-249 as being one of the most exciting non-military tales in Coast Guard enforcement annals. I was glad to do this, partly because it was also a tribute to the bravery of a Secret Service agent who gave his life that others might live.

Since a dedication seems to be appropriate, this book is heartily, sincerely, and cordially

> Dedicated to all Treasury Enforcement Agents,
> whether they be working, retired or on
> some Heavenly assignment.

> Harry Edward Neal
> Assistant Chief,
> U.S. Secret Service (Retired)

CONTENTS

1

ADVENTURE UNLIMITED

The tall man stood motionless among the rocks, looking first at his companions on the right, then at those to his left. The bright Texas moonlight made silvery streaks along the barrels of the revolvers and rifles they carried, and the weapons were pointed at the rickety shack in a clearing some fifty yards away. The men could see an occasional puff of smoke curling out of the shadows near the shack.

"There's somebody in those shadows smoking a cigarette," one man whispered. "Must be their lookout, but I can't see him."

"We can't sneak up on them, that's for sure," the tall man said. "I'll call to them to surrender. If they want to fight it out, let 'em have it. But protect yourselves and don't kill unless you have to. We want to take them back for trial if we can. Okay—spread out and surround the place."

The men crouched low as they took cover behind the rocks. They had tracked this gang of Mexican cattle smugglers to the shack and had gathered enough evidence to

11

put them all behind bars. All that remained was to capture
them.

The leader cupped his hands around his mouth and
shouted into the night, "Hey! You hombres in the shack!
Come out with your hands up! You're under arrest." To be
sure they understood, he repeated the warning in Spanish.

From the spot where the cigarette smoke had drifted
into the moonlight came the sharp crack of a pistol shot.
The bullet went *pinnnng!* as it ricocheted off a boulder.
The lookout dashed out of the shadows, opened the door
of the shack and slammed it behind him.

A moment later there was the tinkle of breaking glass and
more shots came from inside the house. The officers returned the gunfire, and through the night a little war raged
on the Texas plain.

At dawn the leader of the law men was making plans
with his officers to rush the shack, figuring that the outlaws
had little ammunition left and also that some of them may
have been wounded or killed in the fighting. As he was
reloading his revolver he heard a shout from the cabin. He
jumped up and peered cautiously from behind a rock. From
one of the broken windows a hand was waving a dirty white
cloth.

"You give up?" the tall man yelled.

The cloth waved up and down rapidly and a man's voice
answered, "*Si, si!* We give up!"

"Throw your guns out the window," the tall man ordered,
"and then come out the door with your hands up. Savvy?"

Two rifles and four revolvers were thrown out. Then the
door opened slowly and six men emerged. One had a bloody
right leg and limped as he held one arm around the shoulders of a companion. Another held only one arm in the air.
The other hung uselessly at his side, a telltale streak of
blood on his sleeve.

The officers left their stronghold and approached the shack, their guns aimed at the smugglers. As they closed in, the door of the shack banged open and a seventh Mexican leaped into the yard, a six-shooter in each hand. He dashed to the right to avoid hitting his accomplices, then opened fire with both guns. The leader of the law men raised his revolver, took careful aim and shot. The two-gun smuggler cried out once, spun around and fell dead.

The smugglers were jailed and later convicted, putting an end to one of the biggest modern cattle-smuggling syndicates in Texas.

Far from the Texas prairies, on a residential street of row houses in Brooklyn, New York, six men in overcoats huddled together in an automobile at midnight, making a last-minute check of plans for a raid.

Their leader Gabriel Damone wanted to make sure that each knew his role. Damone, a stocky Italian with a small black mustache, had spent twenty-five of his fifty years in law enforcement. Shrewd and fearless, he was calm in emergencies, an able actor in undercover work and one of the best shadow men in the business.

For days he had observed the movements of a suspected counterfeiter named Anello, who lived in one of the row houses near the parked car in which the men now talked. Anello had bought supplies which could be used to manufacture homemade money, and Damone was sure the time was ripe to catch him in the act.

From his inside pocket he withdrew a folded paper—the search warrant which had been issued that afternoon. "Three of us will go to the front door and ring the bell," he said. "If the door isn't opened right away, we'll break it in so they won't have a chance to destroy anything. The other three will go to the back door and wait. As soon as we enter, one of us will go to the rear and let you in."

The three assigned to the back door left the car, the January wind biting their faces. A block away they entered an alley leading to the rear entrances of all the row houses. Because the houses were built wall to wall, and because they all looked exactly alike, the men had to count twelve doors to be sure they had the right one.

Inside the back door was a small cubicle with a furnace and coal bin. This furnace room was dark, but a ribbon of light showed at the bottom of a door to another basement room. The men stood shivering in the night, waiting for their brother officers to enter from the front.

The doorbell rang. Seconds later a woman's voice screamed, "Cops! Cops! Louie—it's the cops!"

Suddenly the men in the alley saw the inside basement door flung open. A man rushed to the furnace, yanked open the firebox door and hurled something into the glowing coals. They could not see what it was.

One of the officers stepped back and kicked the outer cellar door open and the men dashed in. Two sped to the basement and seized the suspect. The third, a young stenographer being trained as an investigator, jumped to the furnace, pulled open the firebox door and closed his hand over the object that had been tossed on the coals. As he brought it out he saw that it was an eight-by-ten-inch photographic negative. Part of the photographic impression had been melted away by the terrific furnace heat, but there remained the clear three fourths of an image of a ten-dollar Federal Reserve note.

The men made a thorough search of the entire house, and although they found printing inks, a press, paper and other counterfeiting materials, they failed to find another piece of incriminating evidence. None was needed, however, because the ten-dollar negative and the suspect's effort to destroy it were enough to convict him and he was sentenced to serve five years in prison.

The young man who grabbed the negative from the coals was soon promoted.*

In the Mississippi swamps two law men tracking a gang of moonshiners had to fight terrific heat, poisonous snakes and stinging insects while plodding relentlessly along a mucky, muddy trail.

Johnny Dixon, one of the officers, was thirty-two years old and had spent seven years learning the tricks of those who made whisky illegally, smashing their stills, and putting the offenders behind prison bars.

His buddy Ralph Jordan had worked in New York and New Jersey, and had only recently been transferred to the Mississippi area. He kept slapping at the mosquitoes that bit his face and neck.

"Are you sure," he said to Johnny, "that we're on the right track? I don't see how anybody in his right mind would set up a still in a stinking jungle like this."

Johnny laughed. "I think my information is solid. And after you work in this territory for a while you won't mind it. It grows on you."

"That's what I'm afraid of. It'll grow all over me."

Suddenly Johnny stopped and put out one arm to halt Ralph. "Wait," he said. He raised his head and began to sniff audibly. "Smell anything?"

Ralph sniffed. "Fermenting mash," he said. "They're around here somewhere."

Johnny spoke in a low voice. "Now remember," he cautioned, "these guys are supposed to be tough. The informant said they'd kill at the drop of a hat, so let's cut the gab and watch our step."

Slowly, cautiously, they squished along the soggy path. Then they both heard a man's voice and a raucous laugh.

---

* The author was the "young stenographer" who recovered the evidence. It led to his commission as a Secret Service agent, culminating five years of on-the-job training.

They moved forward stealthily until they were in sight of a clearing where they saw four men and a moonshine still.

Located on a rise in the ground, the still was in operation. A fire was burning under a huge copper pot with copper coils from which dripped newly made alcohol distilled from the fermented mash. One moonshiner was adding wood to the fire while another sat at the base of a tree, whittling a stick. The other two sat on boxes, talking.

Dixon drew his revolver and Jordan followed suit. Johnny jerked his head toward the clearing and Ralph nodded. With guns ready they stood up and boldly approached the moonshiners.

The man whittling the stick saw them and scrambled to his feet. "Revenooers!" he yelled, and fled through the brush into the swamp. The two sitting on the boxes and the man tending the fire all tried to flee, but collided with each other. One managed to dash away in the direction the whittler had taken.

Johnny fired into the air twice, but the man kept going and soon vanished into the undergrowth. The other two stood with their hands raised until the officers handcuffed them. Johnny took some of the moonshine and mash for use as evidence, then destroyed the still and emptied the barrels of whisky and grain.

The officers herded the captives out of the swamps to the road where they had left their automobile, and started the drive to town. As they rounded a long curve they saw two men with shotguns steps out of the bushes along the highway. Dixon slammed on the brakes. In the back seat with Ralph Jordan the handcuffed prisoners slid to the floor, Ralph keeping them covered with his gun.

The ambushers opened fire with the shotguns, peppering the car with buckshot. The chunks of lead tore through the windshield, some striking Ralph in the chest and shoulder, some lodging in Johnny Dixon's neck.

"No use fighting those shotguns from here," Johnny said. "We're going through. See if you can get a good look at those guys."

He stepped on the throttle and the car leaped ahead. Down the road Johnny and Ralph heard another blast from the rear, but the car was not hit and they delivered their prisoners safely to the jail before they themselves went to the hospital.

They gave good descriptions of the men to other officers, who started a search immediately. They arrested the two men with the shotguns, who had escaped from the still. They were convicted of felonious assault and each was sentenced to serve twenty years in prison.

Many criminals live and work under a lucky star for a time, but sooner or later the star fades and so do they. Such a man was Alejo Danogaro, a dealer in marijuana. For most of his forty-eight years Danogaro managed to keep his wrists out of handcuffs, but his downfall began on a stormy night in Chicago when his henchmen introduced him to a new "customer."

The customer was Vic Doolin, an undercover Treasury agent who had been given one assignment: "Get Danogaro with the goods!"

Frequenting pool halls and taverns, Doolin ingratiated himself with Danogaro's boys, and in time managed to buy small quantities of marijuana from them. On a rainy November night he received a call from "Weasel" Briggs, who was Danogaro's chauffeur and personal errand boy. Vic met Briggs in the latter's hotel room, where the Weasel offered to sell him a small box of marijuana for twenty-five dollars. Vic realized that more small deals would bring him no closer to Big Shot Danogaro, so he complained that the price was too high, the quantity too small. Weasel said he could get pound lots at one hundred dollars the pound.

"How much can you get?" Vic asked.

"All you want. The guy I work for trucks it in from Mexico."

"How long will it take you to get five pounds?"

"I'll have it here at nine-thirty. And you have the five hundred bucks here, too."

Swiftly Vic arranged for two other officers to observe the delivery by the Weasel. In a little while, however, the Weasel came back and said his partner wouldn't trust him to deliver five pounds, and that Weasel and Vic would have to pick it up from "the boss."

In his own car Vic drove the Weasel over the circuitous route to a poorly lighted neighborhood in Chicago. In the darkness and drizzle Vic had one brief glimpse of his brother officers before he and the Weasel went to meet Danogaro. Then the Weasel took Vic to a doorway in a corner building where a dark figure huddled in the shadow. It was Danogaro.

"Stand still and look at me," he said. He lit a match and held it in front of Vic's face—a face that was gaunt and swarthy, with steel-blue eyes. His tough appearance helped to make him a good undercover man.

Danogaro handed Vic a paper bag which Vic took to his car, hoping that other officers would see the sack and make the arrest. Danogaro and the Weasel followed him to the automobile. Slowly Vic counted ten packages of marijuana, each weighing eight ounces. No officers yet. He had to stall, so he felt the weight of each package and broke one open to sniff at the weed. Then he put the bag in the car and asked Danogaro and the Weasel to get in. They refused.

"Just hand over the five C's," Danogaro ordered.

"Okay, okay," Vic said, "but first let's get out of this crummy neighborhood."

"No! I like it here," Danogaro answered. "And you better get up that dough if you want to stay healthy."

Vic shrugged and reached inside his coat as though to

get a wallet. Instead, from his shoulder holster he yanked out his revolver, pointed it at the two men. "This is it, boys. You're under arrest! Stand over there and put your hands on top of the car."

The men didn't move. Warily, Vic shoved Danogaro toward the automobile. The Weasel broke and ran. Vic whirled and fired one shot at him, then saw another officer chasing the Weasel. As he turned back he looked squarely into the barrel of an automatic pistol in Danogaro's hand.

"Drop it!" Vic commanded, his own gun aimed at Danogaro.

"*You* drop it!"

Behind Danogaro another officer came running toward Vic. Danogaro's attention was diverted for an instant. Vic moved—and Danogaro fired. His bullet whistled past Vic's head. Vic dropped him with a shot through the chest.

The agents took Danogaro to the hospital, where he died. A coroner's jury returned a verdict of justifiable homicide and commended Vic for his courage and efficiency. The Weasel was caught and sent to prison.

Not all criminal cases are so dramatic. Some are on the lighter side. In New York City a character who called himself "The Most High" had a long police record for gambling. He dressed in brightly colored suits, always wore a vivid green sash around his waist, and carried what he called a "symbolic" cane. Most of his police arrests had resulted in fines, but the day came when Treasury agents took him into custody for failing to buy a "wagering occupational stamp," as required by federal law.

The agent who made the arrest seized numerous sheets of paper covered with mysterious symbols.

"What are these markings?" he asked. "Policy bets?"

"The Most High" was indignant. "Indeed not, sir," he said. "These markings, as you call them, are notations in the Amharic language. They are my prophecies for my believers.

They are sacred, sir, sacred—and I warn you that if they are damaged or destroyed, great evil will descend upon you and yours."

"I'll take the chance," the agent said. "Get your hat."

While "The Most High" awaited trial, the agent and an expert cryptographer studied the mysterious markings on the seized pages. When the case was called in court they were able to prove that the symbols were not Amharic and were not, in fact, the writings of any religious, ethnic or national group, but were actually records of "numbers" bets in a code invented by "The Most High."

The gambler was sentenced to pay a five-hundred-dollar fine and also to serve a thirty-day prison sentence. When he was being escorted from the courtroom he passed the officer who had arrested him.

"You're pretty lucky," the agent said. "You're getting off easy. How do you feel about it, Most High?"

The gambler shook his head slowly and a faint smile came to his lips. "The Most High is feeling mighty low," he said as they took him away.

Sailors are sometimes good law-enforcement officers. The presence of mind of a young Coast Guardsman, whose real name is John C. Cullen, led to the arrest of several enemy agents who came ashore in the United States during World War II.

On the night of June 13, 1942, the weather was foggy, the visibility very poor, as young Cullen, seaman second class, left the Amagansett Coast Guard Station on the lonely eastern end of Long Island for a six-mile patrol. He had gone only about three hundred yards when he saw three men, one in civilian clothes, the other two in bathing trunks. The man who was dressed was on the shore. The others were in water up to their knees.

"Who goes there?" Cullen called.

The civilian walked toward the sailor. "Halt!" Cullen ordered. "Who are you?"

The man kept coming and Cullen reached for a flashlight in his hip pocket. The man, apparently thinking Cullen was reaching for a gun, stopped and cried, "Wait a minute! Are you with the Coast Guard?"

"That's right," Cullen said. "Who are you and what are you doing here?"

The men in bathing trunks joined their companion and the three approached Cullen in the beam of his light. One was dragging a bag which he said contained clams. Cullen knew there were no clams in the area, but he pretended to believe the man's statement.

"We're from Southampton," the civilian explained. "We were out fishing and our boat ran aground."

"Well, then, come on up to the station. You can have some coffee and wait for daylight."

The man stepped close to the Coast Guardsman. "We do not wish to go to the station," he said in a low voice. He pressed a gun into Cullen's side. "And it is better that I make you forget you saw us."

"What's the idea?" Cullen asked. "What is this?"

The man stepped back. "It is nothing to worry about, my friend. It is just that we cannot afford to have a witness."

Cullen's mind was trip-hammering. Obviously they intended to kill him.

"You don't have to use that," he said. "A little dough might do just as well."

"Dough?"

"He means money," one of the men said.

"Ah, money!"

The three held a whispered conference; then the man in civilian clothes took something from his pocket. "Here's one hundred dollars. Would that help you to forget?"

Cullen didn't want it to look too easy, or to seem too anxious. "Can't you do better than that?"

The man counted out more bills. "How's three hundred?" he asked.

Cullen forced a smile and took the money. Now the fully dressed man put his angular face close to the seaman's. "Look me straight in the eye," he said. Cullen looked. "Would you know me if you saw me again?"

"No. No, I wouldn't."

The man nodded, motioned to his companions and they walked away. Cullen started back toward the station and when he was out of their sight he began to run. He reported his experience to Carl R. Jenette, officer in charge, who telephoned his superiors. Jenette then armed three other men and Cullen with .30 caliber rifles and they hurried to the meeting place, but found no trace of the landing. Off shore, through the fog, the men thought they heard the sound of diesel engines, and Jenette believed he could see the long, thin outline of a submarine, but the noise soon died away.

At dawn they found German cigarettes half buried in the sand, and also a pair of wet bathing trunks. Seeing a place where the sand was disturbed, they dug down and unearthed two heavy and two light wooden cases containing material for making incendiary bombs. In another spot they uncovered two German dungaree outfits, a German overcoat, overshoes and an overseas cap with a swastika.

Coast Guard intelligence officers began an immediate investigation, but had to turn over their evidence and findings to agents of the Federal Bureau of Investigation, who eventually rounded up the Nazi saboteurs.

Had it not been for Cullen's quick thinking, the presence of the spies might have gone undetected, resulting in untold damage to the American war effort.

This and all the other stories you have just read are true. They have been taken from official records of the law-enforcement bureaus of the United States Treasury Department, whose agents are second to none in the grim and dangerous business of fighting crime.

The Treasury enforcement agencies are six in number: The United States Secret Service, the Bureau of Customs, the Bureau of Narcotics, the Intelligence Division, the Alcohol and Tobacco Tax Division (the latter two are in the Internal Revenue Service), and the United States Coast Guard—six against crime.*

This is their story.

---

* Another Treasury agency, the Internal Security Division of the Internal Revenue Service, may be classed as an enforcement agency, but it is concerned primarily with the conduct of Internal Revenue employees and with Internal Revenue administration, and is not, therefore, discussed in this book.

2

ROGUES AND REVENUE

Relentlessly, every day, every night, Treasury agents in the United States and in foreign countries stalk the dope dealer, the counterfeiter, the check forger, the tax cheat, the moonshiner and the smuggler.

The smuggler was among the first of these offenders to feel the teeth of a new law enacted by a new federal government for an old, old reason—the need for money.

The man who sparked the crackdown on pirates who were doing the smuggling was Alexander Hamilton. When Washington was inaugurated as the first President of the new republic, he appointed the thirty-two-year-old Hamilton as his first Secretary of the Treasury. As its name implied, the Treasury was the strongbox, the pocketbook, from which must come the money to finance the operations of the new United States government. Then, as now, this money had to be raised by levying taxes and also by collecting duties on goods brought to the United States from foreign countries for sale to Americans, and even on goods brought from one state to another.

New York, New Jersey and Connecticut placed heavy duties on almost everything. Chicken peddlers from New Jersey lined up at the New York Customhouse to have eggs counted, chickens weighed, duties paid and clearance papers issued. Connecticut firewood was measured, cabbages and turnips appraised. Customs duties, of course, had to be paid on all merchandise.

This situation was changed by the Constitution, adopted in 1789, which provided that "Congress shall have power to lay and collect taxes, duties, imports and excises . . . but all duties, imports and excises shall be uniform throughout the United States."

In 1789 the first Congress under the Constitution enacted a law "for Laying a Duty on Goods, Wares and Merchandises Imported Into the United States." This provided the legal power for collecting duty—but how was the new government going to enforce the law?

For many years before the American Revolution, pirates had plundered ships in the Indian Ocean or off the Atlantic coast of America, and had found a ready market for their loot in New York and New England. The pirates ignored the laws of the colonies requiring the payment of duty, and the merchants were happy to buy the goods at bargain prices. Besides, the pirates purchased other merchandise in the stores, paying in captured gold, so most of the American tradesmen welcomed the business and were not opposed to the widespread smuggling.

Other vessels, not engaged in piracy, also brought goods into American ports and paid little or no duty on their cargoes, depending upon local laws and upon "friendly arrangements" with local authorities—in other words, graft.

On Cape Cod in Massachusetts the "mooncussers" had their own unique methods of acquiring imported merchandise. They would set up fake beacon lights on cloudy or stormy nights, so that ships' captains would be fooled into

steering their vessels upon rocks or reefs. Then they would
loot the wrecks and salvage whatever goods were available,
thus cheating the government, the owners of the ships and
the owners of the cargoes.

The new federal government took a dim view of all of
these operations. Pirates and smugglers were outlaws, plot-
ting to evade payment of duty which they properly and
legally owed to the United States. Shippers considered
reputable should pay their honest debts. Mooncussers were
thieves. President Washington was greatly concerned because a lot of money was needed to operate the government
and it must be raised by taxes and duties. Without money
the new republic could collapse, and all the years of fighting for independence would have been wasted. Washington
and Hamilton talked about this danger and about the new
law requiring payment of duty on imported goods.

"This is a vital source of revenue," Hamilton pointed out,
"and if we don't put a stop to the smuggling, the pirate
trade and other unscrupulous activities, we're lost."

It became one of Hamilton's first jobs to study this problem and to recommend ways to deal with it.

On July 31, 1789, Congress established the federal Customs Service, in which collectors of Customs would accept
payments of duties on imports—but there was still no machinery to halt the smuggling and to make sure that duties
were paid. In October, 1789, Hamilton went to the men appointed as Customs collectors, asking for their opinions and
advice, and more and more he realized that an effective
plan of action would require a small fleet of ships manned by
brave and honest Americans. He reported his findings to
President Washington.

"But we are already heavily in debt," the President told
him. "You're proposing a navy to put down the smugglers,
and at this critical moment we can ill afford a navy."

"This would not be a navy of men-of-war, bristling with

cannon," Hamilton said. "Rather it would be a small fleet of cutters—fast and maneuverable, always ready for action in our coastal waters."

The President agreed to ask Congress for the money and for the authority to build and operate a fleet of small vessels to be used for collecting duties on merchandise shipped from foreign lands. Congress agreed and in 1790 authorized the building of ten cutters for the Treasury's "Revenue Marine." In 1894 this name became the "Revenue Cutter Service," and the organization developed (in 1915) into what we know today as the United States Coast Guard, our nation's oldest seagoing military service.

During its first year of operation the Revenue Marine swooped down on the pirates and others who would cheat the new government, and collected more than two million dollars in Customs duties, proving to the smugglers and to Congress that the nation's investment in law enforcement was more than justified. Equally important was the rescue work of the Revenue Marine, whose cutters helped many a ship in distress and saved countless human lives at sea.

In the years that followed, the Treasury Department continued to be a vital force in the operation of the government. Few people are aware that the Postal Service was supervised by the Treasury until 1829, or that the Land Office (now in the Department of the Interior) was in the Treasury from 1812 to 1849, or that many operations related to business in general were Treasury activities before the Department of Commerce and Labor was established in 1903. The Marine Hospital Service, which later became the Public Health Service, was a function of the Treasury, as was the buying of supplies for government agencies, and (until 1939) the supervision of construction of federal buildings.

In addition to all of these duties, the main job of the Treasury continued to be the collection of revenue to pay for the costs of government, a task which grew more important and more difficult as trade and population expanded. Trade with foreign countries brought more and more ships to our shores that were loaded with goods for American merchants. These goods could not be brought into the country legally without the payment of Customs duty, or revenue. The Customs organization which began in 1789 is known today as the Bureau of Customs, and it is responsible for collecting duties and taxes on imported goods, regulating certain marine activities and preventing the smuggling of merchandise or contraband.

Taxes on rum and other alcoholic liquids produce a large portion of our federal revenue. The first internal taxes were levied in 1791 on distilled spirits (whisky, rum, wine, alcohol) and on owners of carriages. Later the government taxed refined sugar, property sold at auction, legal documents and real estate.

On April 6, 1802, Congress discontinued these taxes and closed the offices of the tax collectors, but when the United States fought England in the War of 1812 the internal taxes were imposed again to raise money for national defense. This time Congress also required license fees to be paid by storekeepers who sold liquor or dealt in foreign goods. Taxes had to be paid on bonds, manufactured goods, household furniture, watches, jewelry and articles made of gold or silver.

These taxes were continued by law until the Civil War began. At that time Congress enacted a whole new series of internal revenue laws to tax almost every kind of business and every source of income, and on July 1, 1862, it created the Internal Revenue Service to collect these taxes and enforce the internal revenue laws.

Today the Internal Revenue Service is the largest single Treasury civilian agency. In addition to many tax collectors, it has an Intelligence Division with numerous investigators whose job it is to track down criminals who try to defraud the government and also to see that all taxpayers abide by the federal tax laws.

One Treasury enforcement agency that is also part of the Internal Revenue Service is the Alcohol and Tobacco Tax Division (ATTD). The ATTD agents administer the internal revenue laws that apply to the making, taxing and distribution of tobacco and whisky, wine, beer or other alcoholic beverages. Every year these agents detect and arrest thousands of people who violate these laws—people, for example, like the moonshiners who make whisky in homemade stills and sell it without paying taxes according to law.

The ATTD also enforces the National Firearms Act, created to prevent gangster weapons such as submachine guns and sawed-off shotguns from getting into the hands of criminals.

Another Treasury enforcement agency whose work is of vital importance to the health and well-being of the American people is the Bureau of Narcotics.

The word *narcotic* is derived from a Greek term meaning "numbness," or "to make numb." A narcotic drug is a substance that numbs the senses. Narcotics are used by doctors and in hospitals to relieve pain or to induce sleep, and when used in this way these drugs are of great benefit to mankind.

Unfortunately, however, many narcotic drugs are used unlawfully in a manner which destroys men and women physically, mentally, emotionally and spiritually. Narcotics such as cocaine, morphine and heroin are habit forming. People who take these dangerous drugs reach the point where they feel they cannot do without them, and the doses must become larger and heavier. In other words, they are addicted—hooked, trapped, even doomed. Such people were once known as dope fiends. Today they are called narcotic addicts, or drug addicts, and they are found in age groups from the teens upward.

The sale and distribution of illicit narcotic drugs are crimes which are fought by the Bureau of Narcotics, organized in 1930 to declare war on the smugglers and pushers (sellers) of contraband dope. With the help of local police and other enforcement groups, the Narcotic agents battle against one of the world's greatest evils, risking their own lives in a dangerous game which gangsters play for keeps.

All of the Treasury agencies we have thus far discussed —the Bureau of Customs, the United States Coast Guard, the Alcohol and Tobacco Tax Division, the Intelligence Division and the Bureau of Narcotics, are responsible not only for enforcing certain federal laws, but also for seeing to it that the government collects revenue which is properly due.

While the collection of revenue is of the greatest importance to the nation, the Treasury has another tremendous and equally vital job—the task of manufacturing money for circulation among the people of the country.

On April 2, 1792, Congress enacted a law to set up a mint for the making of coins. The director of the mint was authorized to produce ten-dollar gold coins (called eagles), five-dollar gold coins (half eagles), and two-and-one-half-dollar gold coins (quarter eagles), as well as silver dollars, half-dollars, quarter-dollars, dimes, half-dimes, copper cents and copper half-cents. In the early days, any citizen could bring gold or silver to the mint and have it struck into coins, free of charge.

The gold, silver and copper coins were an essential part of the country's money supply, but a considerable amount of paper currency was also in use. Before 1863 this paper money was issued—not by the government, but by banks operating under federal or state charters or licenses. Different banks used different designs for their paper money, and the bills issued by a bank in Massachusetts would not look anything at all like those issued by banks in New Jersey or some other state.

This variation in appearance gave a big advantage to a certain type of criminal—the counterfeiter. He could imitate the paper money issued by one bank, then spend it in some other community where a storekeeper, unfamiliar with the design, would not know whether it was good or bad.

At the time of the Civil War it was estimated that about one third of all the paper money in the country was counterfeit!

In 1862 the government was authorized to issue the first national currency, and the federal paper bills, known as greenbacks, were placed in circulation in 1863. The counterfeiters promptly set to work to copy the new money, and in a few months thousands of fake greenbacks were showing up in stores and banks. If the government did not act quickly and decisively, the public would lose all confidence in the federal money and the nation might be thrown into panic or chaos.

Thus, on July 5, 1865, a small force of investigators assembled in the Treasury Department in Washington, where a man named William P. Wood was sworn in by the Secretary of the Treasury as the first chief of a law-enforcement agency which has since won fame and respect throughout the world—the United States Secret Service.

3

SECRET SERVICE

The first task of the United States Secret Service was to drive the counterfeiters out of business. Secret Service agents made wholesale arrests and captured scores of counterfeiting plants, in order to restore and maintain public confidence in the new national currency.

The suppression of counterfeiting is still one of its primary jobs, but in almost a century of fighting crime the Secret Service has sent its men into dangers and adventures that make Hollywood movie heroes look tame. Cases involved a wide range of villains—western gunslingers, hired assassins, kidnapers, swindlers, gunrunners, spies, revolutionaries, land-grabbers, forgers and other breeds of outlaws.

In 1958 Congress was investigating the labor union activities of the Mafia, or "Black Hand," a secret society which began in Italy many years ago, spread to the United States, and which specialized in extorting money from businessmen and others under threat of death. But the Mafia was an old story to the Secret Service. Before 1900 the Secret Service had arrested Blackhanders for counterfeiting and other crimes. In one case a young railroad laborer in New Jersey was murdered by being thrown into a vat of steam in a sugar refinery. Secret Service agents discovered that the killing was engineered by Mafia members of a labor union, who were promptly arrested and later convicted.

In another case the life of Governor Pennypacker of New Jersey was threatened by members of the Mafia. Two Secret Service agents, risking death, located the hide-out of the killers, captured a whole arsenal of firearms, arrested the ringleaders and saved the Governor's life.

The frontier tales of Wyatt Earp, Bat Masterson and other courageous law men were no more exciting than the story of the Secret Service agents who restored order to a small Nebraska cow town terrorized by drunken cowboys on a wild rampage. The government was preparing to prosecute men who had stolen federal lands. The cowboys, sent in by influential ranch owners who might be implicated, scared government witnesses by threatening to kill them if they testified against the thieves. The United States Marshal at Omaha appealed to the Secret Service for help. A group of agents descended upon the frightened town, nabbed the mastermind, and restored peace to the community, all in a single day.

Occasionally we read about plots to smuggle arms and ammunition out of the United States and into other countries for revolutionary purposes. One Secret Service case many years ago shows that this kind of activity is not new. Secret Service agents in New York City, pretending to be rebel sympathizers, spiked a gigantic conspiracy designed to overthrow existing governments on islands from Cuba to Santo Domingo. Not only did the agents arrest the would-be dictator responsible for the plot, but they also seized nearly a million dollars in counterfeit money, some two thousand rifles and two hundred and thirty thousand rounds of ammunition which were destined to be sent to Haiti for a "citizens' rebellion."

In 1898, during the Spanish-American War, Secret Service agents infiltrated a Spanish spy ring, uncovered its headquarters in Canada and exposed the ringleaders, who were banished from Canadian soil.

One of the most dramatic criminal investigations in American history was made by the Secret Service in Florida about 1900. Ignorant German, Polish and Jewish immigrants swarming into the United States were sent to Florida to work in turpentine camps, where they were paid starvation wages and forced to live in dirty, overcrowded hovels. The wealthy Floridians who owned the camps were actually guilty of slave labor practices, and it was the Secret Service which led a probe that ended this sordid slavery once and for all.

In these early years after its founding, the Secret Service was virtually the *only* general investigative agency in the federal government, which accounts for the fact that it was called upon by many different government bureaus for all sorts of assignments. The agency prided itself upon the efficiency of its men and was highly respected everywhere for the success of its investigations. It was to discover, however, that effective law enforcement can suffer when it involves people with power.

In 1906 President Theodore Roosevelt was angered when he learned that millions of acres of government homestead land available for farming in the West were being misused, and he ordered the Secret Service to investigate. A corps of thirty-two agents discovered that powerful western cattle barons were bribing Civil War veterans to file papers for homesteads, agreeing to live on the land and raise crops. Once the papers were approved, the veterans turned the land over to the cattlemen, who not only used it for grazing their steers, but who also cut down trees and dug coal and other minerals out of the ground, leaving stumps and holes which made the land worthless for agriculture and robbed the nation of its natural resources.

The Secret Service agents recovered several million acres of stolen land, and in the course of their investigations they arrested and indicted certain public officials and influential businessmen who had been involved in the land grabs. As a result, Congress decided to take action against the Secret Service by restricting the kind of work it could do.

President Theodore Roosevelt made a strong appeal to Congress in behalf of the Secret Service, but Congress ignored his plea and ordered that its work henceforth be confined to matters relating strictly to the Treasury Department. Accordingly, nine Secret Service agents were transferred to the Department of Justice in 1908 to conduct other investigations, and this force became the nucleus of the organization which later grew into the Federal Bureau of Investigation (FBI).

A brief personal word about the FBI is appropriate here. The FBI today has more than six thousand agents, the Secret Service about three hundred. It is important, however, to point out that the FBI, the Treasury agents and other federal enforcement groups owe much of their success to state and local police departments, and although the police are really the first line of defense against crime, they frequently get little or no public credit for their participation in many important criminal cases.

Obviously the FBI has accomplished a great deal in the law-enforcement field, but it is the author's personal opinion that, man for man, agents of the Secret Service and of the other Treasury enforcement agencies have made greater inroads against crime and criminals and have accomplished more for the American taxpayer than have other federal law men.

Although the duties of the Secret Service were restricted to Treasury matters, there was one task which was not transferred to the Department of Justice and which is still one of the most important responsibilities of the Secret Service. This is the protection of the President of the United States, a duty which began officially in 1901, after the assassination of President William McKinley.

President McKinley was shot while he stood in a receiving line in Buffalo, New York, after he had made a speech there. Among the men, women and children who walked past slowly, shaking hands with the President, was a thin, dark man whose right hand was bandaged with a handkerchief and apparently injured. As he came close to McKinley there was a sharp *crack!* and a puff of smoke from a revolver concealed under the bandage. The President swayed and began to fall. Several men jumped on the assassin, but his work had been done. President McKinley died from his wounds, and the killer Leon Czolgosz was later executed.

The tragedy centered the attention of the nation upon one startling fact. This was the third time in thirty-seven years that a President of the United States had been murdered (Lincoln and Garfield were the other two). This was an average of one assassination every twelve years, while across the seas the killings of foreign rulers were rare. During the one hundred and twelve years between the signing of our Constitution and the McKinley killing, not a single ruler of England, Germany or Spain was assassinated. France, Italy and Austria each escaped with a single victim, while Russia recorded only two instances. True, there had been many attempts at assassination, but they were unsuccessful. Why? Because the heads of European states were given personal protection. The President of the United States, on the other hand, moved about freely without escort or bodyguard, except perhaps at some parade or other public function when soldiers might provide a guard of honor.

After President McKinley's death (and before the crackdown on the Secret Service) Congress called upon it to protect President Theodore Roosevelt and his successors. On June 23, 1913, this protection was extended to the President-elect, and on June 12, 1917, to the members of the President's immediate family. In 1951 Congress authorized the Secret Service to protect the Vice-President if he requested such protection—and Vice-President Richard M. Nixon credited the Secret Service with saving him and his wife from injury or death when they were attacked by howling mobs in South America in 1958.

For many years the Secret Service had the honor of protecting foreign dignitaries who visited the United States, including Sir Winston Churchill, Madame Chiang Kai-shek, Princess Martha of Norway, Queen Wilhelmina and Queen Juliana of The Netherlands, and scores of others. Protection of official foreign visitors is now a function of the Department of State.

Many other special assignments involving physical security were given to the Secret Service because of its expert knowledge in this field. Soon after the Japanese attacked Pearl Harbor in 1941, the Secret Service was ordered to remove certain priceless documents from the Library of Congress in Washington and transport them to a place of safety. The documents included the originals of the Declaration of Independence, the Constitution of the United States, the Gutenberg Bible, Lincoln's Second Inaugural Address and the Lincoln Cathedral copy of the Magna Charta, all of which were later returned to Washington under Secret Service protection.*

---

* With Mr. Archibald MacLeish, then Librarian of Congress, and his assistant Mr. Verner Clapp, the author planned and supervised the removal of these precious symbols of the American heritage.

Protection of the President of the United States involves a great deal more than keeping a Secret Service detail at his side day and night to serve, if necessary, as human shields against bullets or other messengers of death.

When the President leaves The White House, whether to attend a banquet at a Washington hotel or a "meeting at the summit" overseas, Secret Service agents (called the "advance men") precede him by hours or days, as warranted, and inspect the place at which he will appear. They work with local police departments to plan the route by which he will travel; they go over the route themselves, set up a time schedule for his arrival, stay and departure, and lay out a plan for posting agents and police officers at strategic locations along the route and in the building to provide maximum protection.

If the President travels by train, the Secret Service works with railroad police to make sure that tracks are clear, and may even arrange to send a pilot engine ahead of the President's train as an added precaution.

A careful search is made of any building to be visited by the President; and if he is to remain overnight in a hotel, the agents investigate the employees who may have access to his quarters, those who will serve his food, and they also check on occupants of rooms adjacent to those occupied by the Chief Executive.

Sometimes city officials think that the Secret Service uses greater care than necessary in its presidential security plans, but the agency cannot afford to overlook even the most remote possibility of danger. Just after the inauguration of the late President Warren G. Harding, he returned to his home state of Ohio, where arrangements were made to have several thousand well-wishers meet him. Local politicians hired an old steamboat on the Ohio River and decided that the President should meet his admirers on board this vessel.

As usual, Secret Service agents arrived in advance of Harding and were told of the shipboard reception plans. Nearly two thousand people were already aboard the craft, ready to cheer the President. The agents made a thorough inspection of the vessel, then went ashore and shook their heads.

"We're very sorry," they told the welcoming committee, "but this steamer doesn't look safe. We'll find one that's more substantial and in better condition and recommend that the President board it instead."

"But you can't do that!" one committeeman exclaimed. "All these people have been told he'll go aboard this boat."

"We realize how you feel," the agent said, "but we have a job to do and we must do it as we think best. We're sure you wouldn't want any harm to befall the President."

The committeemen continued to protest, but when the President arrived the Secret Service men escorted him aboard a newer boat anchored near the old steamer, where he could be seen plainly by the crowd. The disappointed throng on the older craft jammed along the rail to look across the water at Mr. Harding. Suddenly the entire deck collapsed. The ship seemed to swallow most of the spectators. Screams and shrieks pierced the air. Several people were killed and many were hurt in a tragedy which came dangerously close to bringing injury or death to the President of the United States.

Contrary to popular opinion, the number of Secret Service agents regularly assigned to the "White House Detail" (protecting the President and members of his family) is not great. Normally there are only a few agents with him at all times. If and when he attends some public function, other agents are withdrawn from their regular work in Secret Service field offices to do temporary protective duty as needed.

Protective duty often becomes necessary as the result

of letters written to the President or members of his family. A special branch of the Secret Service, known as the Protective Research Section, has offices in the Executive Offices Building next door to the White House. This section uses a unique system to classify and analyze the many threatening, obscene and abusive letters which are constantly sent to the President. It is important to note that letters of this kind are addressed to *every* president, thus indicating that the letter writers are interested in the office itself rather than the man who occupies it. Some ninety-five per cent of the letters received by the Secret Service for investigation are from people who are mentally disturbed, if not actually insane.

One man in Texas wrote, "I ask you for help now. If you refuse, the day will come when I will have your heart out and I will give it to the ants as food." He was arrested, pleaded guilty and was sentenced to eighteen months in the United States Medical Center at Springfield, Missouri. Soon after his release he was arrested by authorities in another state and committed to a state mental institution from which he escaped twice.

Another threat said, "My duty to the United States is to eliminate you. If God gives me strength, you won't be President long. I will see to that." The Secret Service located and arrested the writer. In court he told the judge that he had meant every word in his letter. After a psychiatric examination showed that he was not of unsound mind, he was sent to prison for three years.

Not long ago a letter addressed to the President, postmarked in Atlanta, Georgia, said: "I have started a new kingdom in Alaska and I am now the King. If you do not make a new state in the Union, you will find yourself looking into a .22 Winchester rifle." The letter, signed "King Harry I of Harrisonia," was turned over to the Secret Service for investigation.

Agents decided that it had probably been written by someone named Harrison. In Atlanta they tracked down the paper on which the letter was written, then located the store where it was bought. After eliminating various suspects, the agents identified the letter writer—a twelve-year-old boy named Harry Harrison (this isn't his real name). It seems that Harry and some of his playmates had each obtained a deed to one square inch of land in Alaska by sending in box tops to a cereal company. They all decided to pool their land and to set up their own new kingdom, whereupon Harry was crowned and then wrote his letter to the President.

The agents talked with Harry's father, a responsible citizen, and together they explained to Harry that he had violated the law by making his implied threat. Harry was pretty scared, but after he found that he was not going to be put in jail he thanked the agents and said, "You don't have to worry any more. I surrender. I'm an American citizen again."

In addition to the Protective Research Section and the White House Detail of agents, a group of uniformed officers, known as the White House Police Force, patrols the White House and the White House grounds day and night. These men, by law, are under the direction and supervision of the Chief of the Secret Service.

The Chief of the Secret Service is appointed by the Secretary of the Treasury. As this is written, this position is held by Mr. U. E. (for Urbanus Edmund) Baughman, and, like others before him, he is a career man, having entered the Secret Service in 1927 as a stenographer and progressed step by step to the top job. Only the thirteenth man to hold this important post, his appointment as Chief was made in 1948, when he was only forty-three years old—perhaps the youngest man ever to occupy that post.

While Chief Baughman, thanks to his practical experi-

ence in the field, made many important improvements in
the administration of the agency, three deserve special
mention. One is the spearheading of a federal law which
defines the powers and duties of the Secret Service. From
1865 to 1951 the Secret Service was granted its authority
from year to year in annual appropriation acts by Congress.
In 1950 Chief Baughman launched a move to get perma-
nent basic legal authority for the Secret Service, and Congress enacted a law in 1951 which sets out clearly the responsibilities of this Treasury agency.

Chief Baughman's second major accomplishment was
the formation of a special training school for Secret Service
agents. For a few years the Treasury Department had operated the Treasury Enforcement Training School in which
investigators from all of the Treasury enforcement agencies
received instruction in criminal law, the laws of search and
seizure, in techniques of surveillance (shadowing), undercover work and other phases of criminal investigation.
This school was necessarily of a general nature, since the
work of the various agencies differed considerably. For that
reason, the Secret Service set up its own academy to give
its agents intense and specialized training in the specific
fields in which they would work—protection of the President, the suppression of counterfeiting and forgery, enforcement of the nation's laws relating to gold, investigations of certain offenses involving the Federal Deposit Insurance Corporation, the federal land banks and other or-
ganizations having to do with the country's financial system.

Chief Baughman's third major accomplishment was the
creation of an inspection system within the Secret Service to insure greater efficiency in all phases of its work;
and also the reorganization of the entire agency to provide
clear-cut lines of authority and achieve maximum production in the most economical manner.

Today, therefore, thanks to Chief Baughman, the Secret Service agent gets not only six weeks' training of a general nature in the Treasury Enforcement Training School, but also studies for five weeks (and later gets advanced and refresher courses) under the guidance of skilled, experienced instructors in the Secret Service Training School. Sample subjects: Counterfeiting Methods and Materials; Detection of Counterfeit Money; Forged Checks and Bonds; Laws Relating to Presidential Protection; Bombs and Explosives; Crowd Control; Recognizing and Handling the Mentally Ill; Analysis of Questioned Documents (handwriting examination, forgery, etc.); Effective Public Speaking; Problems Relating to Administration and Management and many others.

As part of their education the agents get special instruction in such fields as judo, self-defense and first aid, and are taught to use revolvers, submachine guns, riot guns, and other firearms. They are among the finest marksmen in the world. They are also given lessons by competent experts in the dangers of and defenses against atomic, biological and chemical warfare, especially in connection with their responsibility of protecting the President.

Protection of the President and members of his family (probably one of the most important tasks in today's world) is supervised by James J. Rowley, Special Agent in Charge of the White House Detail, a handsome and husky career man whose reputation for courage, tact and efficiency is unequaled.

Although the protection of the President continues to be the Number One security task of the Secret Service, the suppression of counterfeiting and the suppression of the forgery of government checks and bonds are its two major crime-fighting jobs. There are definite ways to detect counterfeit money, and also ferret out some secrets of the inner workings of the counterfeiting racket.

4

HOME MADE MONEY

Counterfeiters have been at work ever since there was a medium of exchange. Emperor Nero, of fiddle fame, is said to have been the first coin counterfeiter. The Pilgrims who came from England on the *Mayflower* and other ships soon learned how to swindle the American Indians by making counterfeit wampum. Napoleon Bonaparte once authorized the operation of a secret counterfeiting plant in Paris, where experts manufactured fake money that Napoleon used to buy supplies for his invasion of Russia. The British made tons of phony Continental currency during the American Revolution, destroying public confidence in the genuine money, and even today we use an expression, "not worth a continental," to describe something as being without value.

During World War II the Nazis, using the talents of expert engravers and printers in their concentration camps, manufactured millions of counterfeit British pounds which

44

actually defied detection. They counterfeited the currency of other countries, too, along with identification and other documents, and they were trying to imitate United States paper money when the Allied advance put a stop to their counterfeiting activity.

There was a time when a counterfeiter had to be a skilled engraver in order to make his printing plates. Today, however, modern photographic processes have simplified reproduction, and most criminals now in the counterfeiting business begin their manufacturing operations by taking a picture of the kind of bill they want to imitate. The picture is developed on a metal plate and then etched with acid.

Of course considerable technical skill is still required to make a good counterfeit bill, and the counterfeiter is thus considered to be a kind of aristocrat of the underworld. He is also one of the most difficult lawbreakers to track down, because everything he does is aimed at concealment; that is, he generally sets up his equipment in some attic or cellar and he is extremely cautious about letting other people know where he is or what he is doing. Usually he has one or two trusted accomplices who can carry away the fake money he prints and sell it at a profit, but the people who buy it from the accomplices do not know where or by whom it is made.

An organized counterfeiting gang operates in a business-like fashion. First there is the maker—the one who holds the plates and manufactures the counterfeit money. He delivers the finished product to a wholesaler.

The wholesaler employs one or more runners (messengers) to take batches of the bills to various distributors.

The distributors, or retailers, sell the bills to passers—the people who will try to swindle small storekeepers by passing the counterfeits as genuine money.

The price of counterfeit money varies according to its excellence and the proximity of the buyer to the maker. A counterfeiter who produces a very deceptive bill may sell it to the wholesaler for ten dollars a hundred—that is, he will sell one hundred dollars in counterfeits for ten dollars in genuine money.

The wholesaler gives the one hundred dollars to his runner, to be taken to the distributor and sold for perhaps fifteen dollars. However, the runner wants pay for his services, so he may add another five dollars to the price, and the distributor thus pays twenty dollars for the one hundred dollars.

The distributor then sells to the passers for varying amounts. If he sells only one or two bills at a time, he may charge at the rate of thirty-five or forty dollars per hundred. If he sells one hundred dollars in a batch, he may charge thirty dollars, pocketing a profit of ten dollars.

The passer, who pays the highest price for the counterfeits, is the one who takes the greatest chance of being caught, so he is as foxy as he can be. Frequently passers work in pairs. One holds the entire wad of counterfeit money, giving his pal only one bill at a time to spend. Generally this bill is put with other (genuine) money in the passer's wallet. Then, if an alert storekeeper or clerk should detect the counterfeit and call a policeman or the Secret Service, the passer can try to convince the authorities that he himself was an innocent victim and that he received the counterfeit in change in some other store. In the meantime, if his buddy, holding the counterfeit bank roll, sees that the passer is being questioned or held, he usually flees to a hide-out or to some other part of town so that he will not be caught with the goods if his accomplice should squeal.

Some crooks have transformed innocent teen-agers into lawbreakers by making them believe that passing counterfeit money is a good way to get rich quick. The passer picks a likely-looking youth on the street and asks him to go into a near-by store and buy a package of cigarettes or some other small item. He gives the boy a counterfeit ten-dollar bill. Suspecting nothing, the boy makes the purchase and returns with the cigarettes and the change. The passer hands him a dollar for the errand.

"Gee, thanks!" the lad says.

"It's okay, pal," the crook answers. "Pretty good pay, huh?"

"It sure is," the boy says.

"I can show you how to make a lot more than that—and just as easily," the man tells him. "You could make maybe twenty, thirty bucks a day."

Naturally the boy is impressed and wants to know more. The man tells him that he has just passed a counterfeit bill, and points out what a cinch it was. He offers the youth a commission to pass other bills, stressing the point that there is no danger, that all storekeepers can afford to take such a small loss, and that if anything should happen, the boy can always "take it on the lam." He fails to explain why, if it's so easy, he doesn't do it himself.

The Secret Service has had many cases in which youngsters have been arrested because they fell into just such a trap. Some have been reprimanded by federal prosecutors; some have been given suspended prison sentences and placed on probation; and others have been sent to federal reformatories. In all such cases, however, the unlucky youth has a black mark against him which may later ruin a promising career, and which will forever be a blot on an otherwise good name.

Sometimes counterfeiters are caught because of unusual circumstances. In New York City an old joke lost all its humor for Robert Mack, who made his own nickels and dimes. The original gag went like this:

He: I put two slugs in a slot at the Automat and
    what do you think came out?
She: I don't know. What?
He: The manager!

When several counterfeit coins were traced to an Automat Restaurant on Forty-second Street, a Secret Service
Agent named Tom Best went there and questioned the employees.

"Of course we only find the coins after the food is taken
out of the receptacles," they told him. "We've never seen
the person who puts them in the slots."

"Think back, now," Tom said. "Is there any one particular
dish the customer seems to prefer?"

The workers shook their heads slowly, then one brightened and said, "Now that you mention it, he always gets
coconut pie."

That evening the agent stationed himself behind the pie
receptacles in the Automat. Coins dropped monotonously
in this slot and that, and the white-coated men and women
were constantly replacing the food in the cubicles. Many
customers bought coconut pie, but paid for it with good
money.

At five minutes past six, three nickels thudded into the
coconut pie receptacle. The agent knew at first glance that
they were counterfeit. With the manager he rushed out
into the dining room, where they found Robert Mack walk-
ing toward a table with his food on a tray.

He was arrested and searched by Tom Best. In Mack's
pockets were twenty-two counterfeit nickels, ten counterfeit dimes, and six metal washers the size of quarters. After
admitting that he had been making and passing coins for
some six months, he was convicted and sentenced.

Most counterfeiting cases are not as simple as this. Some
require weeks or months of hard, boring work—the endless

examination of files and records, the fruitless questioning of people who might furnish leads, the shadowing of suspects, the night-and-day surveillance of a house or a barn or a store, and perhaps the efforts of an undercover agent to infiltrate a gang.

An agent who works under cover may be flirting with death. If his masquerade is discovered, his fate will depend upon his own resourcefulness and quick thinking. If he is dealing with killers, he may expect to be killed or wounded.

In one Pennsylvania case Agent Gabriel Damone succeeded in winning the confidence of a gang of Italian counterfeiters near Scranton. Damone came into the Secret Service from the Pittsburgh Police Department, where he had won a reputation as one of the best detectives on the force. In the Scranton case he was able to arrange to buy fifty thousand dollars in counterfeit ten-dollar bills from Tony Scalzi, a hoodlum long suspected of master-minding various holdups, burglaries and knifings in and around Scranton.

On the night before the counterfeit money was to be delivered, Scalzi met Damone in a small restaurant which they had used several times as a rendezvous. Not far away, other Secret Service men took up inconspicuous posts where they could observe the restaurant, but they did not go in for fear they would make Scalzi suspicious.

Scalzi was very cordial. "I got a surprise for you, Joe." (Joe was the name Damone had assumed for his undercover role.)

"Yeh? A surprise, huh? A good surprise?"

Scalzi laughed. "Very good. You and me—we're going to celebrate."

"That's fine," Damone said, smiling. "What are we celebrating?"

Scalzi registered surprise and held out both hands, palms up. "Our deal! What do you think?"

"Oh, our deal. Okay. That's good, all right. What are we going to do?"

Scalzi stood up. "Come on, I take you for a ride. You'll find out."

Damone followed Scalzi to the door. Had Scalzi discovered his true identity—and was the "ride" to be a one-way trip? The agent could not back out now, and anyway, maybe there was no cause for alarm. Besides, he knew the other agents were keeping him and Scalzi under surveillance, and he took some comfort in the thought.

They entered Scalzi's automobile and drove toward the outskirts of the city. Damone did not want to turn around to see whether or not the agents were following—he merely hoped that they were.

Soon the city lights were behind them and they were in open country. In a few minutes Scalzi slowed down and turned left onto a narrow dirt road flanked by open fields. Instantly Damone realized it would be impossible for the other agents to follow without being discovered, and he knew that they would at least wait until Scalzi's car was out of sight before they attempted to travel in the same lonely area.

Scalzi drove along the dark, rutty road for perhaps two miles before they came to their destination, a farmhouse. Lights glowed from most of its windows, and as they approached the front porch Damone could hear music and the sound of voices from within.

"What's this?" he asked. "Who lives here?"

"My sister and her husband," Scalzi answered, getting out of the car. "Come on, let's go in."

Damone tried to make a quick survey of his surroundings, but the darkness was complete. He could not see the lights of another house anywhere, and there were no woods near by in which his fellow officers might take cover. He knew now that he was strictly alone and on his own.

In the farmhouse Scalzi and Damone were greeted with cheers and laughter by three men and four women. Two of the men were Rocco and Vincenzo, whom Damone had met previously with Scalzi. The other, Ugo, was Scalzi's brother-in-law. He brought Damone a water glass filled with red wine, and held a half-filled one himself. Damone was introduced to the women, none of whom he had seen before.

In the dining room a large table was set. Scalzi had a glass of wine which he clinked against Damone's. "To our big deal, Joe!" he said, and they drank. Then Scalzi pointed to the table. "You see?" he said. "I told you it was a good surprise! We got real good food, none of that restaurant stuff. We got antipasto, minestrone—ah, such minestrone! —spedini, lasagna, spaghetti—everything! The works! All for you, my friend."

Feeling considerably relieved, Damone joked and talked with his hosts. Before the dinner was served, he saw one of the women whisper something to Scalzi, who went with her into the kitchen. A few minutes later Scalzi emerged and went directly to Damone. Scalzi's eyes were cold and angry. In a low voice he said, "Joe, I want to talk to you. Private." His strong fingers grabbed Damone's arm and guided him into the kitchen. There Damone saw the woman who had whispered to Scalzi.

Scalzi let go of the agent's arm. "Go ahead," he said to the woman. "Tell him what you just told me."

She stepped nearer and faced Damone, a sneer on her lips. "Your name ain't Joe," she said. "You're Gabriel Damone. You're a cop from Pittsburgh. I seen you there in court once."

A hundred thoughts bubbled through Damone's mind and burst. There was no time to think, for if he groped for a defense he would surely betray himself.

Calmly he stared at the woman and at Scalzi, and a grin grew into a chuckle as he began to stroke his black mustache with one finger, first on one side, then on the other.

"I knew I should have shaved off this mustache," he said. "This is the third time I've been mistaken for that cop. I guess I must look something like him, all right, but it's the mustache that does it. He's got a mustache like mine, hasn't he?"

The woman nodded.

"You say you ain't Damone, huh?" Scalzi demanded.

"Tony," the agent said with a tone of disgust, "you ought to know better. I've never even seen the guy. Besides, if I was a cop in Pittsburgh, what would I be doing here in Scranton? Would I have come out to this place with you—alone? You know about my connections in New York—and here, look at my stuff." He pulled out his wallet and began laying cards on the table, a driver's license, membership cards, a Social Security card—all in his assumed name. He glanced at the woman. "I don't blame her, though. I told you I've been taken for this cop before. Look," he added, hiding his mustache with one finger, "now do I look like him?"

The woman took two or three steps to the right, then to the left, her eyes intent upon the agent's face and figure. Finally she looked at Scalzi, shrugged and made a face as though to say, "Maybe I was wrong."

"Is it him or not?" Scalzi asked.

The woman picked up some of the identification cards and examined them closely. "I could have sworn it was him. But it was seven years ago I seen him."

"Yes or no?" Scalzi growled. "This is important, Maria!"

After another glance at the smiling—and anxious—Damone she said, "No. I guess I didn't remember so well. I'm sorry, Joe."

So the dinner went off as planned, and the next afternoon Scalzi delivered the fifty thousand dollars in counterfeit bills to Damone. The instant the package changed hands Damone placed Scalzi under arrest and signaled other agents, who came to his aid.

An angry Scalzi spat at Damone. "I should have listened to Maria last night," he said. "If I had believed her, you would be where you belong—buried in the pigpen on the farm."

Scalzi and his accomplices went to prison for several years, causing a lot of passers of counterfeit money to lose a good source of supply.

The passer of counterfeit money trades on one important fact: He knows that most storekeepers can't tell a good bill from a bad one. Can you? You can if you will do a little studying of genuine money.

Every counterfeit bill is a *copy* of a genuine bill, but no copy can be exactly like the original in all respects. It's even impossible for you to write your own name in exactly the same way twice! The Secret Service points out that if people would take time to study and examine their money, the counterfeiter would have a hard job spending his fakes. Here are some tips about what to look for in detecting a bill believed to be counterfeit:

The Portrait: This is the oval picture in the center of the face of every bill. It is very difficult for the counterfeiter to reproduce without ink blotches or other defects. The GENUINE portrait stands out distinctly from the fine screenlike background. The eyes in the face are bright and lifelike. On the COUNTERFEIT, the screen background is usually dark, with broken lines, and some of the tiny squares are filled with black ink. Often the picture in the oval merges with the background and does not stand out clearly

The Seal: Every genuine bill carries the Treasury seal in blue, green or red. On the GENUINE bill the sawtooth points around the rim of the seal are clear and sharp. On most COUNTERFEITS the points are blunt, rounded or broken off. The color may also be poor.

Serial Numbers: Every genuine bill has eight serial numbers (plus two letters), printed in two places on its face. On the GENUINE these numbers are uniform in size, are printed evenly and are well-spaced. On most COUNTERFEITS, some of the numerals may be thick or thin, may lean to the left or right, and may be unevenly spaced. Like the Treasury seal, they may differ in color from the genuine.

The Paper: The paper on which our genuine money is printed has many small red and blue threads scattered through it. Most COUN-TERFEITS are printed on ordinary bond paper without colored threads, although sometimes counterfeiters actually draw red and blue pen-and-ink lines on the paper to imitate the genuine threads. GENUINE currency paper has no watermark, but occasionally a COUNTERFEIT is printed on watermarked paper.

Some people still believe that if you rub a dollar bill on a piece of white paper and the color rubs off, the bill is counterfeit. This is completely false. Rubbing a bill on paper proves nothing whatever—the ink can be rubbed off good bills as well as bad ones.

Coins are also counterfeited, though not too extensively, since the profit is not as great as that from phony paper money. Most counterfeit coins today are made of inferior metal in plaster molds. In one Secret Service case a little boy went into a grocery store to buy a loaf of bread. He gave a quarter to the grocer, who dropped it on the counter, noticing immediately that it sounded more like a button than a coin. He examined it closely and said to the boy, "Sonny, this coin is no good."

With wide eyes the youngster looked at him and answered, "Oh, it must be good, mister. My father just cooked it!"

Dropping a coin on a hard surface, as the grocer did, is only one way to detect a counterfeit. A genuine silver coin rings like a bell, whereas most counterfeits sound dull and flat.

Many counterfeit coins feel greasy to the touch.

Look at the outer edge of a silver coin and you will see a series of corrugated ridges, known as the "reeding." On a genuine coin these ridges are parallel and evenly spaced. On most counterfeits they are crooked in some places, perhaps missing entirely in others.

If you should receive a counterfeit coin or bill, put your initials and the date on it (for future identification) and deliver it right away to your police department, your bank, or to the nearest office of the Secret Service, with all the information you have as to where it came from.

If you work in a store and a customer gives you a counterfeit coin or bill, try to think of some natural excuse to get him to wait—then telephone your police department and report the counterfeit. A police radio car can usually respond to your call in one or two minutes.

If the customer leaves before you can call the police, try to see whether or not he gets into an automobile; if he does, *write down* the license number and give it to the police or the Secret Service with the customer's description.

The fact that most of us rarely give a second look to the money in our pockets is really a great tribute to the Secret Service, which keeps counterfeiting at a minimum. However, the person who gets stuck with a bad coin or a bad bill may be a person who suffers some hardship from his loss, so learn to look at the money you receive and you won't be fooled by counterfeiters—not even by expert counterfeiters like Luke Redden, for example.

5

LUKE THE LONER

Luke Redden, a tall, gaunt Swede with sorrowful gray eyes, first came to the attention of the Secret Service in 1927 in Detroit, Michigan, when he tried to pass a counterfeit five-dollar bill in a grocery store. When he was questioned by Secret Service agents, this skinny bachelor with the bloodhound face, who carried an umbrella over one arm, claimed he did not know where he received the fake bill. Unfortunately for him, however, he had two others just like it in his wallet, and the agents promptly informed him that they were going to search the furnished room where he lived.

"Well, then," Luke said mournfully, "I guess you'll find everything you want. It's all there—the plates, the press, everything."

He was right—it was all there—and it was all seized. More questioning revealed that Luke was a "loner"—he had no accomplices; in fact, he had no friends. For months he had studied books about photoengraving and had experimented in making plates until he was capable of producing better-than-average counterfeit bills. What made his work distinctive, however, was the fact that he actually manufactured his own paper on which the bills were printed. The method he used will not be revealed by the Secret Service, which has no desire to educate other would-be counterfeiters.

Luke was not especially greedy, he said. He didn't seek to get rich by passing his counterfeits; he merely wanted to live comfortably. He had worked as a waiter, a carpenter, a bricklayer, a plasterer, an upholsterer and a camera repairman, and it was in the latter job that he became interested in the counterfeiting venture. The way to make money, said Luke, was simply to make money!

Luke pleaded guilty and ambled out of the federal courtroom to live in prison for three years.

In 1938 certain storekeepers were victimized by new counterfeit five-dollar bills which the Secret Service had not seen before. Experts in its Counterfeit Section compared the workmanship on this new counterfeit with that of known counterfeiters, finally concluding that the bill had been made by Luke Redden. With the help of technicians in the analytical laboratory of the Bureau of Engraving and Printing, where our genuine paper money is made, they discovered that the paper on which the counterfeit was printed was unlike paper that could be bought in stationery stores, and this confirmed their belief that Luke had returned to his old trade of do-it-yourself money-making.

The word went out to Secret Service field officers: "Find Luke Redden!"

This, the agents were to discover, was to be no easy job, for Luke Redden had disappeared, vanished, evaporated.

There were few leads the Secret Service could follow, but agents tackled them all. Luke had no dependents, no known friends. He did have two sisters whose names and addresses were known to the law men, and the agents kept their homes under surveillance for a time, thinking that Luke might be living with one of them. He wasn't. The agents then talked with both sisters, who claimed that they had not heard from their brother and did not know where he could be found.

The Secret Service knew that Luke had used other names, and these names, together with his picture and description, were sent to police departments all over the country, asking that the Secret Service be notified if Luke was located. Result? Negative.

Luke's counterfeit five-dollar bills kept appearing in Chicago, Kansas City, St. Louis, New York and other cities, but they were not detected as counterfeits until they had been deposited in banks by the storekeepers who accepted them—and most of the storekeepers could not remember what the passer looked like. A few were of the opinion that the bills might have come from a tall, sad-looking man wearing baggy clothes, who walked with a kind of shuffling movement. When they were shown Luke's photograph, they promptly identified it as a picture of the passer. In other words, Luke was once more working as a lone wolf, making his counterfeit money and passing it, too. He was also doing considerable traveling.

The agents buckled down to do the hard, tedious kind of investigating that has no glamour, no excitement, no fascination—the drudgery of down-to-earth detective work. They checked the records of waiters' unions, carpenters' unions, unions representing other trades at which Luke had worked. Nothing. They exhausted all the leads they could think of, including a careful review of the file relating to his arrest in 1927, more than ten years earlier. Nothing.

From 1938 to 1948 Luke's counterfeit notes kept bobbing up here and there—only a few at a time, but enough to let the Secret Service know that their fugitive was still a firm believer in do-it-yourself.

One day an agent called on one of Luke's two sisters to ask more questions. No, she hadn't yet heard from Luke. No, she had no idea where he was. Yes, if she heard from him she would let the agent know. This didn't fool the agent one bit.

Leaving the sister's home, the agent called on the sister's husband at his place of business. No, he didn't know where Luke might be. He didn't know much about Luke at all. He did remember that Luke once told him he had bought two building lots somewhere near Chicago and was thinking about selling them because he had no automobile and they were difficult to reach by bus.

Again the agent talked with the sister. Did she know where those lots were located? Sorry, no. She knew Luke had bought lots, but he had said only that they "were near Chicago."

This was the first new lead developed in the ten-year search, and the agents bore down on it. They questioned dozens of real estate dealers in Chicago, seeking records of any transactions with Luke Redden or any of the other names he was known to have used.

In one office, as an agent looked on, a realtor searched index cards bearing the names of his clients. He had none of the names the agent had furnished, but the agent noticed one card with the name "Leonard Randall." These were Luke Redden's initials—"L. R."—and Leonard Randall was the owner of two lots near Grayslake, Illinois. Just recently the firm had received a letter from Mr. Randall saying that he would soon send them money which was still due on the lots. There was no return address on the letter, but the envelope bore a Chicago postmark.

Now the agents added the name "Leonard Randall" to their list of aliases and leads, and their first move was to search the Chicago telephone directory. There they found a listing for "Randall, Leonard," and another for "Randall Studios," each with the same address and telephone number.

At the address given they saw a second-floor window in a two-story building with the gold-lettered words, LEONARD RANDALL—PHOTOGRAPHS. This, at last, could be pay dirt.

They set up a watch on the building. Sure enough, that very morning they saw Luke Redden, fugitive counterfeiter, come out of the street entrance and shuffle away. The agents followed him to an artists' supply store and saw him emerge carrying a small package. As he headed back toward the studio, one agent shadowed him while the other checked in the store. Luke, he discovered, had just bought a can of printer's ink, of a color known as bank note green.

Back at the studio the agents still did not take Luke into custody. First they wanted to learn more about what he was doing. The next morning Luke was seen to come out of the building and empty a bag of trash into an ash can. As soon as they could, the agents examined the trash and inside the folded pages of a copy of the Chicago *Daily News* they found a torn-up piece of blotting paper about four by eight inches, with traces of green ink. As they assembled the torn bits like a jigsaw puzzle, they saw a green rectangle the size of the back of a five-dollar bill, and they could even see the blurred outline of a big numeral "5" in one corner!

Armed with this evidence, the agents obtained a search warrant and with the special agent in charge of the Chicago Office they sped to Luke's photograph studio. They did not rush in at once. At exactly 4:40 P.M. they saw Luke come out and walk to the corner, where he bought a newspaper. He ambled back to the building, and as he approached the entrance the agents began to converge on him.

Luke trudged up the worn stairs, glancing back just once

at the men who were unhurriedly climbing the steps behind him. He went directly to his studio, took a key from
his pocket and unlocked the door. As he went in, the agents
were close on his heels. They closed the door and only then
did Luke take a good look at them through his spectacles:

"Hello," he said.

"Hello, Luke," one answered.

"Can I do something for you?" Luke asked.

"I guess you can," the supervisor said. "You can show us
where you keep your counterfeiting plant. We're from the
Secret Service."

"Oh." There was a long pause. "May I see your identification?"

The agents produced their credentials and Luke examined them with care. Then the special agent in charge
took the search warrant from his pocket and began to read
it to Luke.

"Never mind," Luke said, waving a bony hand. "You
don't have to go through all that. I've been expecting you.
What you're looking for is in here." He showed them two
metal foot lockers, one in his reception entrance and one
under the bench in his darkroom. Both chests were locked,
and Luke took keys from the top of a small wall cupboard
and opened them.

The lockers contained plates for the counterfeit five-
dollar bills he had been passing, as well as partially com-
pleted plates for new five- and ten-dollar bills which he
was planning to print. His printing press was a hand-type
clothes wringer which he had bought from a mail-order
house.

"I'm glad it's all over," Luke told the agents later. "I
knew you were looking for me, and every time I heard a
step on the stairs I figured you'd caught up with me." He
rubbed his stomach gently. "You fellows didn't do me any

good, you know, worrying me like that. I've got a very troublesome ulcer."

Once again Luke pleaded guilty in federal court, but this time the judge was not as lenient as before. Luke and his ulcer were sent to prison for fifteen years, with the understanding that when he is released (probably in 1960) he will be deported to Sweden.

In prison Luke will associate with other counterfeiters who were foolish enough to believe that they could compete with the Bureau of Engraving and Printing or the United States Mints (in San Francisco, Denver and Philadelphia), and not get caught. He will also meet specialists in another crooked field, the forgery of government checks—"scratch men" who have one thing in common with Luke. They were also arrested by the Secret Service.

6

THE MAN WHO TOOK
THE TREASURY

In a recent year the Federal Bureau of Prisons reported that there were more check forgers in federal prisons than any other class of lawbreaker. The Secret Service receives from 30,000 to 40,000 forged government checks for investigation every year, and every year its agents send hundreds of forgers to jail.

A great many government checks are stolen from mail boxes at private homes and apartment houses—checks which were issued for Social Security benefits, veterans' pensions, retirement, income tax refunds and other purposes. The thieves steal the checks, endorse them in the names of the rightful owners and then cash them in stores by posing as the persons named on the checks. Many merchants, anxious to make a sale, do not want to antagonize customers by asking for good indentification, so the thieves have little difficulty in cheating such timid storekeepers. Any honest stranger who seeks to cash a check in a store certainly expects to be asked to identify himself and is glad to do so.

One of the most unusual forgery cases in Secret Service history began in 1954, when the Veterans Administration in Washington reported to the Treasury Department that somebody had cashed a government check for ten thousand dollars. This in itself might not be so unusual—but it appeared that the endorsement on the check had been forged, and that the check was actually cashed right in the main Treasury Building in Washington!

The check was payable, let's say, to one Frank A. Polk. The name "Frank A. Polk" had been written on the back of the check, which also bore a single fingerprint in the lower left-hand corner. In addition, there was a Treasury Department rubber stamp and the initials of a teller in the Treasury's Cash Division, where many government checks are cashed for federal employees.

Secret Service agents interviewed the teller and his supervisor. The teller said the supervisor had authorized him to pay out the ten thousand dollars for the check. The supervisor declared that the check was brought in by a man about forty years old and about six feet tall, who asked if he could get it cashed. The supervisor, noticing the large amount of money involved, suggested that the man take the check to some bank and open an account with it. The man thanked him and left the Treasury.

A couple of hours later the same man returned with the check and talked again with the supervisor.

"I took it to a bank," he said, "but they told me that it would take several days for me to draw any money against the check, because it would have to clear in the regular way. I couldn't wait that long, because I'm having some serious family trouble and I need several hundred dollars for an emergency."

The supervisor, sympathizing with the man, asked him

for indentification. He produced a Veterans Administration building pass and some correspondence addressed to "Frank A. Polk," the name on the check.

If the supervisor had any suspicions at all, he brushed them aside with the reassuring thought that no crook would be foolish enough to ask the Treasury itself to cash a government check if anything was wrong with the check. He authorized payment, and the teller shelled out ninety hundred-dollar bills and one thousand dollars in fives, tens and twenties. The man thanked them, pocketed the small fortune and walked away.

The real Frank A. Polk, who never received the check, was questioned at his home in North Carolina, and here the agents learned how a simple mistake by the forger had uncovered his crime. The real Mr. Polk was expecting his ten-thousand-dollar check (as the result of the death of his son, a member of the armed forces), and the check was properly due him. When it did not arrive, he wrote to the Veterans Administration and he received this reply:

Dear Mr. Polk:

This has reference to the payment of insurance benefits based on the service of your son, Johnny Polk.

It has been found necessary to contact the Department of Defense for more information. Normally this requires 30 to 60 days, at the end of which time full payment will be made to you.

This delay is deeply regretted and you may be assured that upon receipt of this information your claim will be expedited and you will be notified as quickly as possible.

The signature on the letter proved to be a forgery, also, and the forger had written the letter to allay any suspicion on the part of Frank A. Polk. The crook's biggest mistake, however, was in writing the name on the envelope. The letter itself was properly addressed to Frank A. Polk—but the envelope bore the name of Mr. William A. Polk. When it was delivered to Frank A. Polk he thought it might be for someone else, so without opening it he marked it to go back to the Veterans Administration. It was there that the letter was found to be a fake—and a search of the files showed that a ten-thousand-dollar check had already been issued to Frank A. Polk and mailed in care of a small hotel in Washington, D.C.

The Secret Service men questioned the hotel manager, a woman.

"Yes," she told them, "Mr. Polk registered as being from the War Department. I remember, because he had no baggage and said he merely wanted a place where he could relax, and he gave me one week's room rent in advance."

Did she remember whether or not he had received a government check?

"Oh," she said, "that was funny. When he registered he said he was expecting an important piece of mail and asked if I was holding anything for Frank A. Polk. Then I remembered that a government envelope had come in earlier that very morning—but since there was no Mr. Polk registered here, I gave it back to the mail carrier. When Mr. Polk asked about the letter, I told him what had happened and he asked if I would try to get it back, so I telephoned the post office and told them Mr. Polk was here. They brought the letter back and it was delivered to him. If that was the check you're talking about, he got it, all right."

Working with Veterans Administration investigators, the Secret Service agents began to piece together a peculiar puzzle. The check for ten thousand dollars was issued to Frank A. Polk as an insurance payment, but before such payments can be made, several vouchers and printed forms have to be drawn up and signed and approved by VA officials.

The Secret Service men located the signed and approved vouchers and forms in the Polk case, and then searched for the typewriters on which they had been prepared. Surprise! The important voucher—the one authorizing the payment—was not typed on any machine in the Veterans Administration. Furthermore, the signatures and initials on the voucher were out-and-out forgeries. But they must have been forged by someone who knew the routine.

Once again came the dreary task of digging, digging, digging. The agents questioned all VA employees who had access to the Polk papers, or who had anything to do with the case, but they failed to turn up any worth-while leads.

An effort was made to classify the fingerprint on the back of the check, but the impression was not clear enough to be classified.

For more than two months the agents probed, questioned and double-checked without result. It began to look as though the forger had succeeded and would never be identified. Then one afternoon Agent Danny O'Driscoll (this *is* his real name because he deserves full credit for a good job) sat reading the file over and over, seeking some new trail to the forger; but there was none and Danny knew it, for he had thumbed through the reports and correspondence many times before. He sat back in his chair, gazing out of the window.

Suppose I were the forger? he thought. Suppose I had ten thousand dollars in cash in my pocket. What would I want to do with it? He turned this over in his mind several times. I might start by buying a new car, he thought. Then, Well? What about him? Maybe that's what he would do, too! It was a big "maybe," but there it was. Danny took his idea to his special agent in charge, who agreed that it might warrant investigation even though any successful results were indeed remote.

First, arrangements were made with the District of Columbia Motor Vehicle Bureau to permit agents to search its automobile registrations during the week end. Then the Secret Service collected specimens of the forger's handwriting—the hotel register signature, the forged signature on the VA letterhead, the forgeries on the VA vouchers and forms and the endorsement on the forged check. Since there was some variation in all this writing, the agents made a composite picture combining all important characteristics of penmanship.

Armed with this composite for comparison purposes, four agents worked in the License Bureau throughout Saturday and Sunday, examining thousands of automobile registrations, looking for an unknown signature which resembled the handwriting of their specimen. In searching seven thousand five hundred files they pulled out ten registrations of possible suspects. Gradually these were eliminated until they had only one left—the one that most nearly resembled the forged endorsement on the check. This was a registration for a Pontiac Catalina coupé bought from a Washington dealer on May 20—just one day after the check had been cashed in the Treasury Building. The owner's name was given as Lester P. Scott, with a Washington address. He had paid $3060 in cash for the Pontiac.

Agents sped to the address given on the registration, a rooming house, only to learn that Scott had moved away on June 16, leaving no forwarding address. The landlady did not know where Scott worked, whether or not he was married, whether he owned a car.

At the Pontiac dealer's where Scott bought the automobile, the agents learned that he had brought in the car on June 15 for the new-car 1000-mile inspection, although the odometer showed that it had been driven only 574 miles.

At the Veterans Administration they learned that Lester P. Scott was a former VA employee; that he had been married and separated from his wife; and that he had received a disability discharge from the Army, in 1945, for flat feet.

New developments came quickly. The agents were able to learn that the fingerprint on the forged check appeared to be the same as Scott's right thumbprint in his army file.

They located his estranged wife, who said she had seen him occasionally and that on June 22 he had told her he was driving someone to California. The "someone," Mrs. Scott believed, was a redhead named Martha, a waitress in a Washington restaurant frequented by Scott.

The restaurant proprietor said that on June 22 Martha had loaded her personal belongings in a "flashy new car" parked in front of the place and had told him she was going "back to California." He said she had often spoken about returning to her home there. He also furnished an address where Martha had lived in Washington with a close friend.

Under a pretext the agents interviewed the close friend, who said Martha was living on Cedar Street in Glendale, California (she gave a street number). A teletype was flashed to Secret Service agents in Los Angeles, who rushed to the address and learned that Martha was unknown there.

The Pontiac dealer in Washington then reported that the car sold to Scott had been serviced at a Pontiac agency in Glendale, California, on June 29. The California agency had no address of the car owner. It appeared conclusive, however, that the suspect was in the Glendale area.

Now came a startling discovery. The Veterans Administration learned that *another* check for $10,436.40, payable to one Wallace Docker, had been processed fraudulently, just as the Polk check had been. The Docker check had been deposited in a Washington bank on June 15, and the account was closed when the entire amount was withdrawn on July 7. The handwriting on the Docker check was unquestionably Scott's.

This presented a real puzzle. The Secret Service was reasonably sure that Scott was in California on June 29, when his car was serviced there. But he must also have been in Washington on July 7, when he closed his account at the bank.

The agents checked all airline offices in Washington, and at American Airlines they discovered that Lester P. Scott had left Los Angeles for Washington on July 6 and had flown back to Los Angeles on July 7. Swiftly the Los Angeles Secret Service office checked with American Airlines there and learned that the flight reservations had been made by telephone from an address on East Chestnut Street, Glendale.

This address proved to be a small bungalow occupied by a family named Worcester. By careful inquiry of neighbors, the agents learned that the Worcesters had recently been visited by relatives from Washington and that these relatives had moved into a house on Chevy Chase Drive in Glendale.

The agents took up a watch at the suspected address on Chevy Chase Drive. Soon after midnight on August 27 they saw a Pontiac Catalina with a California license pull up and park. A man and woman got out and started for the house. From the descriptions the agents were sure the pair were Scott and Martha, and the two were immediately taken into custody and admitted their identities.

Scott confessed that preliminary work on the two claims involved had begun while he was still a VA employee, which is how he knew of their existence. He said he had stolen blank forms from the Veterans Administration and had prepared them on a typewriter in the restaurant where Martha worked. One evening at closing time he entered the deserted VA offices and substituted his fake vouchers for the real ones covering the two insurance checks, forging the necessary signatures and initials of approval. Then he attached notes to each showing that the checks were to be mailed to the Washington addresses where he later received them. Through his previous employment he knew exactly how to process the vouchers and where to place them so they would be put through routine channels without further question. On VA stationery he had sent the phony letter to Frank A. Polk to keep Polk from making inquiry about the check.

Scott surrendered $2,204 in cash. Some of the money from the checks he claimed to have lost in a betting spree at a Delaware race track. Some he used to buy his automobile. He claimed he gave about $10,000 to Martha to purchase a liquor store in Burbank, California, but she denied it, insisting that the store was bought with her own funds and with money borrowed from her sister. Her sister corroborated her story and Martha was not prosecuted.

Scott was sent to prison for three years and his car was forfeited to the government. He was fined $2000 and ordered to pay the United States the sum of $6393.93 plus costs of $311.50.

This is the story of the man who took the Treasury—and vice versa. Not all forgery cases involve such excellent detective work as this one, and very few forged checks are for such large amounts. The majority of such checks range from $50 to $150 and are much easier to negotiate. Checks have been stolen by children to buy candy and toys, by women to buy new clothes, by men to use for gambling —but perhaps one of the most vicious reasons for check-stealing is the terrible craving of the narcotic addict for heroin, cocaine and other illicit drugs. Many addicts must pay as much as $75 or $100 a day to satisfy their habit, and are thus driven to check-stealing and other crimes to get the needed cash.

The fight against the drug racket is waged by another Treasury enforcement agency, the Bureau of Narcotics—and a fierce and dramatic battle it is.

7

THE DOPE RACKET

Every year thousands of human beings all over the world commit murder, assault, robbery and other crimes because they have poisoned themselves with the juice of a beautiful flower, or an extract from a tropical shrub, or with smoke from a dried weed.

The flower is the opium poppy.

The shrub is the coca plant.

The weed is marijuana.

The human beings are drug addicts.

Here is a dictionary definition of the word *drug*: "A substance (other than food) that, when taken into the body, produces a change in it. If the change helps the body, the drug is a medicine; if the change harms the body, the drug is a poison."

And here is the definition of an *addict*: "A person who is a slave or a devotee to a habit."

Opium (from which we get the word *opiate*, meaning "a drug to ease pain or bring sleep") is produced from the juice of the opium poppy "fruit," or seed capsule. It is, in fact, the source of some thirty or more alkaloids, including two highly dangerous drugs—heroin and morphine.

The leaves of a coca plant, or shrub, produce cocaine, another substance which can harm the body, and which man has tried unsuccessfully to make synthetically.

Marijuana (or marihuana), a kind of hemp, is known in various parts of Asia and Africa as bhang, or as hashish (or hasheesh). Early in the eleventh century a Moslem sheik named Hassan-Ibn-al-Sabbah set himself up as grand master of a new secret order to support a religious sect known as the Ismailites, dealers in mysticism and miracles. Hassan's plan to help the sect was simple: Kill its enemies.

It was not easy, however, to convince his recruits that murder was all in the day's work; so as part of their training Hassan required them to chew hashish or to drink a brew made from the plant. For a time the drug induced pleasant dreams, and the sheik convinced the "students" that these dreams would become reality "in Paradise" as long as they obeyed his commands without question. Thus, stupefied by the drug, their normal thinking twisted and misted, the smokers killed on order; and because of their use of hashish they came to be called hashashins, meaning hashish-eaters, from which comes the word *assassin.* This is the same drug we know as marijuana, also called "tea," "hay," or "Mary," used in cigarettes known as "reefers" or "sticks" and smoked by many young people who learn too late that the reefer-fire will ultimately destroy them as it destroys all sense of time and space and the cigarette itself.

Opium is also used for smoking, and with similar harmful results. Probably no one knows when opium was first used to ease pain or to intoxicate. Records tell us that some two thousand years before Christ the ancient Egyptians invaded poppy fields at night to cut the unripened seed capsules of the flowers and collect the brown, gummy juice.

They used it as the principal ingredient in a pagan punch, ignoring the unpleasant fact that the poppy juice smelled like rotten potatoes, gave the habitual user a deathlike pallor, deprived him of his appetite, reduced his frame to skin and bones and frequently drove him stark, raving mad.

Unlike marijuana, opium is not smoked in a cigarette. A small piece of the drug is "cooked" or roasted over the flame of a special lamp, and the smoker then inhales three or four puffs through an opium pipe made especially for the purpose. At first it acts as a stimulant and fatigue-killer, but its increasing use "hooks" the smoker so that he cannot do without it, even though he comes to realize that he is slowly and surely destroying his mind and body.

Many years ago opium was used in the United States for all sorts of ailments. It was an important part of the contents of many patent medicines which any customer could buy in a drugstore without a prescription. Consequently, more and more people became addicted to its use without realizing the harm that was being done.

In 1853 came the invention of the hypodermic needle, followed by the discovery of morphine as an opium derivative. Injected by needle, morphine acted swiftly and was considered the most effective of the known painkillers. In addition, doctors at first believed that it could cure opium addiction and that in itself it was not habit forming, so they administered it to opium users to help them shed their habit. Instead, of course, the patients contracted a new and worse addiction. Many were given hypodermic needles and taught to take their own morphine shots. The drug was used extensively in treating wounded soldiers during the Civil War, and it was not until 1870 that the medical world realized that morphine was so dangerous its use must be restricted. By that time, of course, hundreds —or perhaps thousands—of soldiers and others had innocently become addicted to its use.

Now the opium poppy gave up one of its most vicious secrets—heroin, perhaps the most dangerous of all narcotic drugs. Heroin, sometimes known in the underworld as "H" or "horse" or "white stuff," is a poison which is a contraband drug in the United States. Commercial use of heroin was begun by the Germans in 1898, when once again doctors believed it to be a nonhabit-forming "miracle drug" that could cure addiction to both opium and morphine. Within four or five years it was clear that heroin was the worst drug of all, as far as addiction was concerned, and by 1914 the world's physicians considered it wise to stop the manufacture of heroin. Within those few years of its use, however, the underworld had discovered that this drug could bring fancy prices from those who craved it, and that dealers could cheat by secretly mixing pure heroin with sugar, powdered milk, chalk or other substances, making a small quantity larger and more profitable. An ounce of heroin costing perhaps sixty to one hundred dollars abroad, might be so adulterated in the United States that it would make enough to be sold for six to eight thousand dollars!

To increase the trade, the dealers or "pushers" often agreed to give an addict a free supply of heroin if the addict would persuade a friend to take his first "joy pop." Sometimes, too, a confirmed addict or "junkie," deprived of all sense of moral values, found that he could no longer associate with decent people. Craving companionship as well as drugs, his solution was to make other men or women sink to his level by introducing them to the narcotic—with the assurance that all the stories they might have heard about "dope fiends" were the bunk and that they could quit whenever they pleased.

In this way addicts made addicts and business boomed for the drug dealers. The average cost of addiction is about ten dollars a day, but the confirmed addict might spend anywhere from fifty to one hundred dollars a day to satisfy his craving. Addicts in the United States spend about four hundred million dollars a year for narcotics. In order to get this money they resort to virtually any kind of crime or violence, for without the drug they would suffer the most excruciating physical torture, perhaps ending in death.

We have seen how Mother Nature has, by a flower and a weed, furnished the materials to do untold injury to man. She has also brought forth a tropical shrub—the coca plant —which man has used to add to his miseries, for this plant gave him his first taste of another body-punisher—cocaine.

The shrub originated in Bolivia and Peru and was later cultivated in Java. Peruvian natives were known to chew its leaves to ward off weariness and also in the belief that it would increase their strength; as with any narcotic, however, its constant use often resulted in failing health and mental deterioration.

In 1859 an Austrian scientist isolated cocaine alkaloid from the coca leaf, and within the next few years doctors became aware of the effects of cocaine as an anesthetic. Unfortunately, since they had not yet learned to be cautious in the use of all narcotics, they discovered the sad truth that cocaine was another powerful habit-forming drug which users took in tablet form, by sniffing the powder ("snow"), or by hypodermic injection. Cocaine is no longer used as an anesthetic since newer drugs, such as novocaine (a synthetic), are effective and far less dangerous. Also, cocaine and morphine are in less demand by addicts than heroin, marijuana and opium.

Opium smoking, contrary to popular belief, did *not* originate in China; in fact, their desire to combat this vice led the Chinese into war. Opium was imported into China from India, and its use spread like the plague it was. Soon the Chinese began to grow the opium poppies for their own use, and in 1729 Emperor Yung Chen tried to restrict the crop for the good of his people.

Seeing a way to make considerable money, the British and Dutch began to ship opium into China. The Chinese authorities seized large shipments of English opium and as a result China was attacked by Great Britain in the so-called Opium War of 1840. China lost the war, but she continued to refuse to legalize the use of opium among her people. Smuggling continued to such an extent that in 1855 the opium traffic led to another war, with China on one side, Britain and France on the other. The outcome was different this time, for China was compelled to permit the cultivation of opium as well as its importation from India.

The Chinese government kept up its opposition, and in 1907 entered into an agreement with India whereby China would forbid the growing of opium poppies and India would gradually reduce the quantities of opium exported until, after ten years, the shipments would stop entirely. For several years the agreement worked satisfactorily, but in 1917, when it appeared that China might have the problem licked, a Chinese political upheaval blasted any such hope, and the opium traffic again blossomed and thrived.

Other countries knew that China would need help to stop the opium traffic, and in 1909, upon a suggestion of President Theodore Roosevelt's, a commission with representatives from thirteen nations met at Shanghai and drafted recommendations to control opium distribution. These recommendations led to the International Opium Convention of 1912 at The Hague, the first real international effort to fight the traffic in opium, morphine and other narcotics. The convention was ratified by the United States and sixty-nine other countries.

The United States had already taken steps to fight the drug racket by enacting a law on February 9, 1909, to forbid other nations from shipping opium and its derivatives into this country, except for medicinal purposes, and absolutely forbidding the importation of smoking opium. After the 1912 convention, another American law prohibited the exporting of any opium or cocaine or derivative, except to a country which regulated the entry of such drugs.

On December 17, 1914, the Harrison Narcotic Law was enacted, requiring all persons who manufactured, imported, sold or otherwise dealt in opium or coca leaves, or any preparation thereof, to register and pay an occupational tax. Enforcement of this law was originally the job of the Internal Revenue Service, and although it was an internal revenue measure, the law actually limited the availability of narcotic drugs to medical and scientific uses only.

Other United States laws, such as the Narcotic Drugs Import and Export Act, approved May 26, 1922, clamped down more vigorously on the importation of narcotic drugs, except for medical needs, and led to an important change in enforcement.

Enforcement of the federal narcotic laws remained with the Internal Revenue Service until 1930, when Congress realized that a separate agency should be created, devoted exclusively to the control of the drug traffic. Accordingly, Congress established the Bureau of Narcotics in the Treasury Department on July 1, 1930, and President Herbert Hoover appointed Dr. Harry J. (for Jacob) Anslinger of Altoona, Pennsylvania, as Commissioner of Narcotics. Commissioner Anslinger, one-time foreign service officer, delegate to various international conferences on smuggling and alcoholism, and former Assistant Commissioner of Prohibition, was ideally suited to the new post, which he has held since it was created. He was later appointed as the United States representative on the United Nations Commission on Narcotic Drugs, and in 1957 was made chairman of that commission.

The Treasury Building, with statue of the first Secretary of the Treasury, Alexander Hamilton.

resident Truman signs the bill defining the powers and duties of the U. S. Secret Service, July 16, 1951.
eft to right: E. H. Foley, Under Secretary of the Treasury; Don Hansen, Asst. to General Counsel; U. E.
aughman, Chief, U. S. Secret Service; Harry E. Neal, Secret Service; James J. Rowley, Special Agent in
harge, White House Detail, USSS; Gerald Behn, Ass't. Special Agent in Charge, White House Detail,
USSS; Seated with President, Secretary John Snyder.

Secret Service Chief U. E. Baughman presents a gold Secret Service badge to retiring Assistant Chief Har
Edward Neal as Secretary of the Treasury George Humphrey looks on.

slow procession, Secret Service Agents walk beside the President's car, flying the stars and stripes and the President's flag.

Secret Service Agents are skilled in the use of all types of firearms.

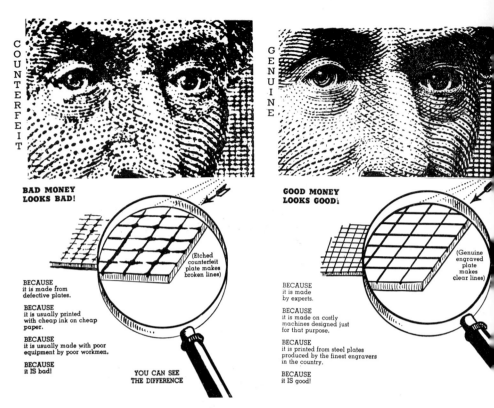

COUNTERFEIT

BAD MONEY LOOKS BAD!

BECAUSE it is made from defective plates.

BECAUSE it is usually printed with cheap ink on cheap paper.

BECAUSE it is usually made with poor equipment by poor workmen.

BECAUSE it IS bad!

(Etched counterfeit plate makes broken lines)

YOU CAN SEE THE DIFFERENCE

GENUINE

GOOD MONEY LOOKS GOOD!

BECAUSE it is made by experts.

BECAUSE it is made on costly machines designed just for that purpose.

BECAUSE it is printed from steel plates produced by the finest engravers in the country.

BECAUSE it IS good!

(Genuine engraved plate makes clear lines)

How to tell the difference between good and bad money.

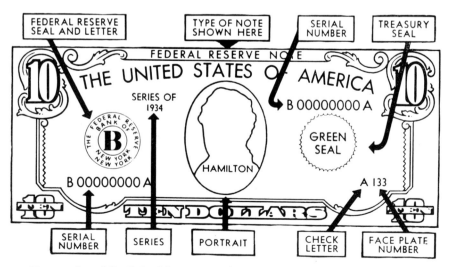

FEDERAL RESERVE SEAL AND LETTER

TYPE OF NOTE SHOWN HERE

SERIAL NUMBER

TREASURY SEAL

FEDERAL RESERVE NOTE

THE UNITED STATES OF AMERICA

SERIES OF 1934

B 00000000 A

GREEN SEAL

HAMILTON

B 00000000 A

A 133

TEN DOLLARS

SERIAL NUMBER

SERIES

PORTRAIT

CHECK LETTER

FACE PLATE NUMBER

Diagram of ten dollar Federal Reserve note, showing important features of paper money.

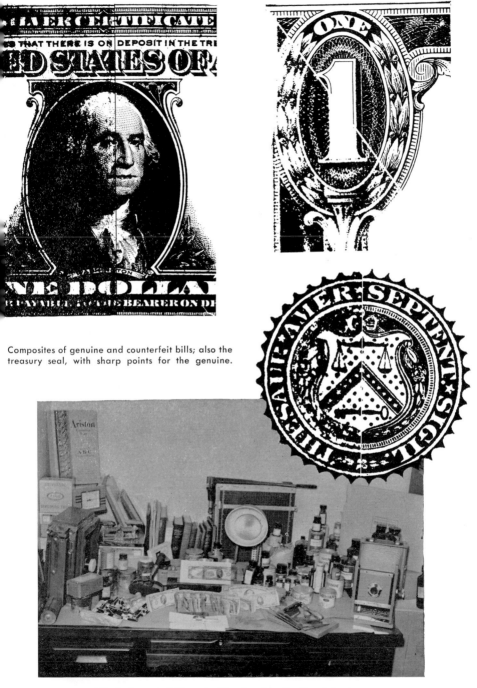

Composites of genuine and counterfeit bills; also the treasury seal, with sharp points for the genuine.

Typical counterfeiting plant captured by the Secret Service.

Pot-type still located in swampy area.

Typical small pot-type still seized by agents. "Pot" was made from two wash boilers.

1500 gallon metal still captured in a wooded area in the south.

Modern cutter used by the Coast Guard for its port security and search and rescue work.

Gunnery practice is important in the patrol work of the U.S. Coast Guard.

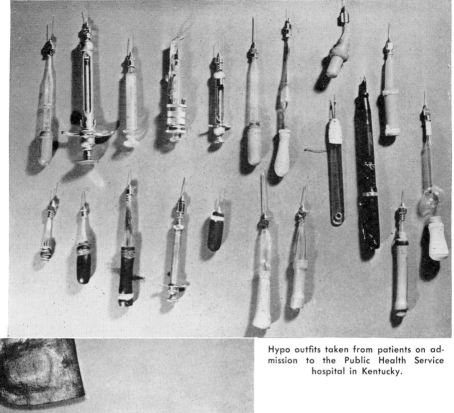

Hypo outfits taken from patients on admission to the Public Health Service hospital in Kentucky.

Narcotic concealed in the heel of a shoe.
←

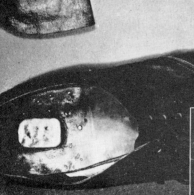

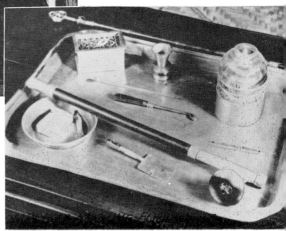

Complete outfit for smoking opium.

Modern methods speed up customs clearance at Idlewild Airport, New York.

Customs officers examine baggage of ship's passengers arriving at an Eastern United States port.

A carved wooden golden pheasant, made in Japan. The bird is hollow and the plug shown on the table fit into an opening directly under the tail.

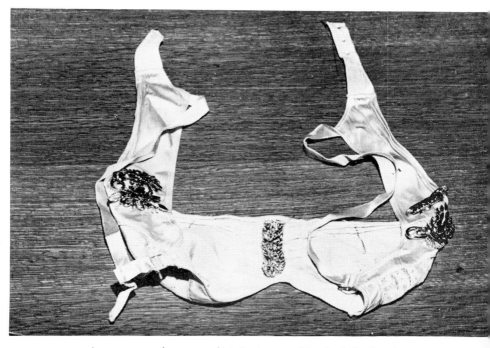

A woman smuggler was caught trying to conceal jewelry in her brassiere.

Customs agents arrested the smuggler who tried to hide these watches by sewing them to a corset-like belt.

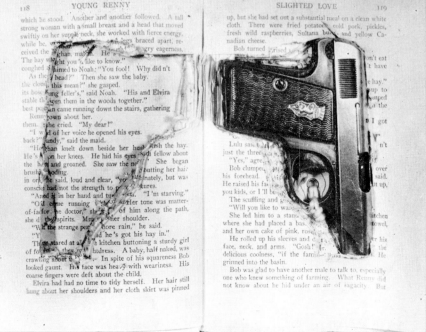

A seaman failed to fool the customs men with an old trick—cutting book pages to hide a gun.

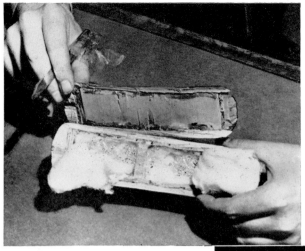

Diamond smugglers hollowed out the top of a clothes brush to hide their gems but the agents had seen that trick before.

A typical trick—trying to smuggle "Decks" of opium ashore in packs of cigarettes →

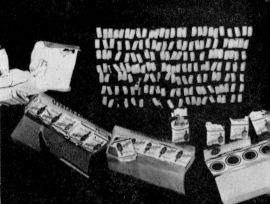

Customs agent examines 48 pounds of gum opium which smugglers tried to hide in the spare tire of their car.

Firearms and military supplies destined for rebels in Cuba were captured by customs men in the U.S.

A hollowed out telephone book concealed drugs.

Customs inspectors remove gold bars hidden in fender of car being shipped abroad.

A shipment of pearls discovered under the false bottom of a trunk.

These watches were hidden in hollowed-out boards, as shown.

A smuggler's vest was made for carrying gold bars.

Marijuana was concealed in the smuggler's boots.

Bomb carrier developed by the secret service to transport bombs and explosives with maximum safety.

Commissioner Anslinger's first blows were aimed at the overseas sources of supply of illicit narcotics. Most of the marijuana comes from Mexico. Raw opium is smuggled from India, Pakistan, Iran, Hong Kong, Red China and Mexico. Heroin is sneaked in from Lebanon, Turkey, Iran, India, Yugoslavia, Red China, Burma, Thailand, Hong Kong and France. Raw opium for legitimate purposes is imported into the United States only from Turkey, Iran and India, in amounts decided upon by the Bureau of Narcotics after consultation with the United States Public Health Service, and distribution is strictly controlled.

Commissioner Anslinger's earlier foreign service was of immediate value, since it enabled him to develop sources of information abroad concerning shipments of smuggled drugs. Within two months after his appointment, Narcotic agents and agents of the Bureau of Customs in San Francisco boarded a steamship from the Orient and seized three hundred five-tael tins of smoking opium (a tael is an East Asian unit of weight equal to about one and one-third ounces avoirdupois), which were packed in sacks and hidden under a cargo of hemp rope.

Two months later a squad of Narcotic and Customs agents in New York City seized twenty-five cases, labeled Furs, as they were unloaded from a steamship out of Istanbul. Instead of furs, the cases contained 17,500 ounces of contraband morphine.

The Bureau of Narcotics teamed up with the Bureau of Customs in searching other suspected vessels and unearthed more large shipments of drugs intended to be sold in the American underworld. Next, Commissioner Anslinger cracked down on the domestic drug traffic, and in 1931, the year after his appointment, 3128 violators of the narcotic laws were convicted and sentenced to a total of 9866 years. Scared whispers echoed through the dives and dens of the dope dealers: "Don't deal with anybody you don't know—and even if you know 'em, be careful. Your own mother might turn out to be one of Anslinger's agents!"

Like the other Treasury enforcement men, Anslinger's agents take danger in their stride. One of the wildest gun battles in the city of New York was fought between Narcotic agents and the crew of a Greek steamer docked in the Hudson River.

Undercover agent Ralph Peters struck up a friendship with Sabbas Tunis, one of the ship's officers, knowing him to be a suspected dope dealer. After Peters bought two or three small quantities of opium, Tunis agreed to sell him a sizable amount of opium, heroin and cocaine.

On the September night when delivery was to be made, Peters led a raiding party to the pier, where they watched the ship for Tunis' signal. Near the bow a flashlight blinked four times.

"Two of you come with me," Peters said. "The rest of you be ready to pounce."

The three agents walked up the gangplank, where Tunis was waiting. "Who are they?" Tunis asked, pointing to Peters' companions.

"A couple of my partners," the agent said. "I told you I'd bring them, remember? You think I'd come down here alone with all this dough in my pocket?"

In the darkness the agents could see members of the crew standing in various places around the deck.

"Let me see your money," Tunis said.

Peters took a roll of bills from one pocket and handed it to the Greek. "This is only three hundred," Tunis told him. "Where's the other seven hundred?"

"Right here," Peters answered, producing a wad of bills from another pocket. Tunis glanced at the handful of money and turned toward his crew, saying something in Greek.

One of the agents with Peters understood the language. "Watch it!" he shouted. "They're going to rush us!"

Swiftly Peters drew his revolver. "All right!" he cried. "We're Treasury agents and you're under arrest!"

A pistol shot cracked near the bow and the bullet thudded into something behind Peters. Peters returned the fire. More shots came from other directions and men began to shout. Suddenly a searchlight beam swept the deck as a small boat approached.

"It's the Harbor Police!" someone yelled. "The cops!"

The sailors began to close in around the Treasury agents. Some of the crew held clubs or iron bars. They shouted as they clashed, and the agents were swinging fists and using the butts and barrels of their guns. Police officers from the Harbor Patrol and the other agents on the pier came clambering over the side and joined the fracas, while a few of the crew members took cover and began to shoot into the tangle of bodies. There were fiery flashes from the guns of the police officers and Treasury men, and the buzz of bullets seemed to be everywhere.

Suddenly a man's voice shouted in Greek and the crew began to flee through the open hatches. The officers quickly followed, but the ship's passageways were dark and some of the pursuers were ambushed in the unfamiliar labyrinth below decks. Others stalked the prey, and this was when the officers' training in judo, disarming and self-defense paid off. One by one the crew was rounded up. Many had been wounded in the gun battle, but all of the agents and the police officers escaped with only a few bruises.

Agent Peters and his men searched the ship, capturing three hundred pounds of raw opium, heroin and cocaine—a bonanza in the illicit market. The agents won a well-deserved commendation from Commissioner Anslinger.

Harry Anslinger is visibly disturbed about the teen-agers who are trapped by drug addiction. "It cannot be too strongly emphasized," he says, "that the smoking of the marijuana cigarette is a dangerous first step on the road which usually leads to enslavement by heroin."

Just what are the physical effects of drug addiction? "In the early stages," Commissioner Anslinger explains, "the addict's breathing and pulse rate are slowed down, blood pressure is reduced and body temperature lowered. His eyes are reddened, his pupils pinpointed and his eyelids droop. He may suddenly become very active physically and then become drowsy and inactive and may drift into light sleep, suddenly awaken, and then drift back to sleep and have fantastic dreams—dreams which might be most unpleasant. He may also suffer from dizziness."

This is merely the beginning. What follows is perhaps the most agonizing experience in human misery. "When he can't get the drug," the Commissioner goes on, "he becomes very uneasy. His eyes water as though he had hay fever, he yawns, mucous runs from his nose. Soon his muscles start to twitch violently and his back, arms and legs ache severely. He has violent pains in his stomach, he vomits, has diarrhea, kicks his legs and jerks his arms. He curls up in bed or on the floor and puts on as many blankets as he can find, even in the hottest weather. His feet twitch continuously. If he sleeps at all he is extremely restless. Finally sleep becomes impossible. He can't retain food or liquor in his stomach, so he loses weight rapidly—as much as ten pounds within twenty-four hours! He may have the illusion that bugs are crawling over his skin. About the third day without the drug he is in the very depths of torment—yelling, screaming, ready to do anything, no matter how terrible, to get the drug. He is unkempt, disheveled, dirty, no longer caring about personal cleanliness, and he has lost all sense of decency."

According to the Commissioner there are many so-called "smart" people who think they know more than the doctors about narcotic drugs, and who decide to "experiment" just to see what an excursion into dreamland is like. These people become addicts just as easily as any others, and their dreamland turns into an unbearable nightmare.

Addiction also breeds crime. "A young person who gets into addiction," Commissioner Anslinger points out, "is sleepy most of the time. He becomes poor in his studies and has no interest in athletics. He is irritable, tells stupid lies, or refuses to talk at all because he is completely preoccupied with himself. His addiction usually results in a career of crime, simply because the addict is too sleepy and unreliable to hold a legitimate job, although he needs an enormous amount of money to keep himself supplied with the increasing quantities of the drug he craves."

How do most young people get started on the addiction route? "Ordinarily," the Commissioner says, "they are tempted first with a marijuana cigarette. A boy may not even know he is smoking dope, but once he is addicted it becomes easy to try a little heroin. Some teen-agers are 'dared' to try the 'stuff.' Some think they can handle anything, but they're so wrong. They can't fool with narcotics. Nobody can. I have one important word of advice for your readers. *Never let anybody, for any reason, persuade you to smoke even one marijuana cigarette. It's pure poison!* The only way to keep from ending up as a drug addict is to use common sense and never even begin. Once you decide to 'experiment' you are headed for a living death."

To fight the "living death" the Bureau of Narcotics has about three hundred Narcotic agents, including a few who are assigned to foreign countries. Because this is such a small force it centers its work on wholesale dealers in illicit narcotics and on major investigations. Most of our metropolitan police departments have so-called narcotic squads of detectives whose job it is to choke off the dope traffic in their own cities and also to work closely with the agents of the Bureau of Narcotics. Without police help, the task of the Bureau of Narcotics and all other federal law-enforcement agencies would be exceedingly more difficult than it already is.

Many Narcotic agents have an attribute which is common to agents in the other Treasury enforcement agencies—they are first-class actors. Their roles are of much greater importance than those of any Hollywood stars, for they play the parts of drug addicts, thieves and murderers, and they must do it well because they play for keeps. These are the undercover men, and for one of them to step out of character at the wrong time might well mean the final curtain.

Consider the time that an undercover agent, using the name of Benny Vitteri, acted his way into a dope ring to negotiate for a "buy" of ten thousand dollars' worth of narcotics. The ringleader Sam Milano ran a shooting gallery in Santa Cruz, California, as a cover for his dope deals. Benny made his entrance by doing a little shooting at the gallery, where he struck up an acquaintance with Milano. A friendly chat broke the ice, and after several more visits the two were almost as close as brothers.

Sam boasted about his cleverness and finally introduced Benny to his friend "Big Ears" Tony Galappa. Big Ears and Sam entertained the agent, who let it be known that he might be interested in buying illicit drugs. While the deal was still in the talk stage, Big Ears took a ride one night with "persons unknown" and he never came back. Later the car was found with pieces of Big Ears on the front seat.

The case developed more angles than an octopus has tentacles. One led to a mob in New York City which had been headed by a notorious gangster deported to Italy. Others involved distributors in New England, boat operators to and from the Bahamas and Haiti, and an underground route from Mexico for smuggling Mexican opium and heroin. One of the Mexican operators was tabbed as a suspected associate of Sam Milano, but when the time came to close in, the Mexican's body was found near Tijuana. He had been shot through the heart, his throat cut and his skull bashed in.

The murders of Big Ears and the Mexican gave undercover agent Benny an unmistakable idea of the ruthless tactics of the gang he was out to trap. While he continued to negotiate with Milano for a buy, a gangster called "The Eye" arrived from New York, saying that he was in California for a vacation. Actually, though, Benny learned that he had come to buy twenty thousand dollars' worth of dope from Milano to take back to New York.

About six hundred and twenty-two ounces of opium and eight ounces of morphine were packed in two suitcases. The Eye was to leave the following day. Sam Milano and The Eye, however, didn't trust each other, so they elected Benny, the undercover agent, to be custodian of the drugs for the night!

Benny was in a tight spot. He couldn't act without prematurely exposing the government's hand. Furthermore, after his all-out performance to convince Milano that he, Benny, was a drug dealer, if he now attempted to reveal his true identity and seize the narcotics, it was probable that Milano and The Eye would conclude that he was hijacking the shipment for himself and that they would try to kill him for it.

Such a moment is fraught with danger for every undercover man. Ordinarily he carries no credentials while on undercover work, and he spends days, weeks and even months posing as a criminal to gain the full confidence of a gang. When he may be forced to end the masquerade in a few tense seconds, to make a seizure and an arrest, it is easy to understand that those who have accepted him as a member of the mob find it hard to believe he is "the law." Lawman or crook, however, the moment comes when he is suddenly an enemy, and in the dope racket enemies are often permanently "eliminated."

This was the situation confronting Benny, and he decided to sit tight until the next morning, when he watched The Eye depart with the drugs. Then Benny telephoned other agents, who nabbed The Eye in the railroad station at Chicago, with the two suitcases containing the narcotics. The Eye was sent to prison for ten years, Sam Milano for twenty.

Perhaps one of the most incredible cases in the entire history of the Narcotics Bureau was that of an addict we'll call Howard Oakes.

The Oakes case was assigned to Agent Jim Fredericks, who had investigated other cases involving the illicit sale of drugs by doctors—and Oakes was listed as a doctor. The one mistake in his fantastic career was that he wrote too many prescriptions for narcotics and aroused the suspicions of a druggist in Flint, Michigan. The druggist reported his suspicions to the Bureau of Narcotics and Fredericks took up the trail.

First he wanted to check into Oakes's background. He examined Internal Revenue Service records to be sure that "Doctor" Oakes was registered there, as the law requires. It turned out, however, that the number used by the doctor was registered to a druggist in Detroit!

Fredericks made inquiries of other druggists in Flint, and other doctors, and apparently one of the people to whom he talked had warned Oakes that he was under investigation, for when Fredericks went to Oakes's offices and home, he discovered that Oakes had made a hasty departure for parts unknown.

A neighbor had seen a truck from a local storage company take some baggage away from Oakes's home. At the storage company Fredericks learned that the baggage had been left by Oakes, with instructions to hold it until he sent for it. The agent arranged to be notified if and when the storage company heard from Oakes, and he then began an intensive investigation into Oakes's personal history. The facts were almost unbelievable.

Oakes had been a radio repairman until 1943, when he took a job as laboratory technician in a private hospital in Detroit, a job requiring no great skill. He read medical books for six weeks, then told the doctors he wanted to work with them as a doctor. He was twenty-five years old. The doctors laughed, Oakes insulted them and was fired.

The trail now led to another Detroit hospital, to which Oakes had gone as soon as he lost his laboratory job. There he told the doctors that he was a third-year medical student of Washington University in St. Louis. He was hired as a laboratory technician and learned a little about X-ray work, but after one month he quit and went back to his original trade—repairing radios.

In 1945 he showed up at a hospital in Flint, Michigan, again posing as a third year medical student. He was hired—and this time he made blood counts, urinalyses, tested blood smears and throat cultures.

Unable to sleep one night because of a pain in his leg, Oakes took a dose of dilaudid, a narcotic drug.

"I liked the effect of it," he said later, "and I began to take it regularly."

Soon the dilaudid seemed weak, so he switched to morphine. To get the drug he wrote fake prescriptions for hospital patients and used the dope himself, or else he stole quantities of morphine tablets from the hospital stock.

Now Agent Fredericks uncovered the most incredible part of Oakes's career. Leaving the Flint hospital, Oakes went to Windsor, Canada, where he convinced doctors that he was a physician and surgeon, and he persuaded hospital authorities there to hire him as a house doctor. He actually diagnosed cases, prescribed medicines, attended childbirths and performed autopsies. In the operating room he assisted with appendectomies, leg amputations, gall bladder removals and skin grafting. And all the time he continued to take morphine. Oakes was now a confirmed narcotic addict.

In July, 1946, he became acquainted with an elderly Flint physician who was so ill that he could not maintain his practice, and Oakes inveigled the sick man into letting him take it over.

His first act was to take the old doctor's diplomas from the office walls, paste his own name over the originals, then take them to a shop where he ordered photocopies made. The photographer seemed curious about the pasted slips bearing Oakes's name.

"Oh, that," Oakes said. "You see, when they made out my diploma they printed my name in Latin, but I wanted it in English, so I pasted the English over the Latin. Otherwise, people might not know it was me!"

He hung the photocopies on the office wall so that patients could see they were dealing with a genuine physician.

In his spare time Oakes sometimes donned a uniform and posed as a former army colonel, one-time flight surgeon of the famed Flying Tigers. He bought an airplane and after only three hours of dual-control flying he made his first solo flight. During his career he owned three planes and was adjudged by fliers who rode with him to be an expert pilot—but he never held a pilot's license.

This was the man Fredericks now sought. All leads ran into blank walls until one day the storage company received a letter from Oakes requesting that his baggage be sent to a certain Detroit hotel. Fredericks and other agents went to the hotel and found Oakes, who was arrested without difficulty. His baggage held a large assortment of medicines, two hundred surgical instruments, stethoscopes and other hospital equipment.

Oakes was sentenced to serve two years in a federal prison. The sentencing judge, amazed by the defendant's fantastic history, said, "I warn you not to try to pose as the prison doctor while you are in jail."

The only surgical work Oakes performed behind bars consisted of an attempt to cut his way out with a hacksaw, for which he was sentenced to an additional year.

To get a more detailed picture of investigative methods used by the Bureau of Narcotics, Commissioner Anslinger has permitted us to look at a file in a closed case with an international flavor. This isn't a highly dramatic shoot-'em-up crime story. Instead, it attempts to show real-life Narcotic agents in a rather typical example of the kind of public service in which they risk their lives every day.

8

TRANSATLANTIC TRAP

Agent Jacques Chandon of the Bureau of Narcotics sipped his black coffee as he waited in the small "coffeepot" restaurant on Atlantic Avenue in Brooklyn, New York. He looked again at the clock on the wall. It was almost midnight. Maybe the deal wouldn't go through. Maybe the Weasel was suspicious, after all. Maybe Jacques hadn't been as convincing a dope dealer as he thought, in which case George Maskedon, the Weasel's "connection," would refuse to meet Jacques and the case would blow up before it even got started.

At 11:47 P.M. Jacques saw the Weasel through the restaurant window, motioning to him to come outside. He rose leisurely and sauntered out. Across the street he caught a shadowy glimpse of another agent—one of a team keeping him and the Weasel under surveillance. He followed the Weasel into a dark doorway where the Weasel took from his pocket a square of napkin paper folded into a packet about twice the size of a postage stamp, then handed it to Jacques.

"I saw the old man," the Weasel said, "and I told him you were hot for a deal. He had two Egyptians there and they gave me this sample of heroin to show you. I told them that if it was okay, you and I would meet them right away to talk business. Okay, Jack?"

The undercover agent was relieved. His audition had been satisfactory and the play had now begun.

At the old man's house Jacques met George Maskedon, who introduced his Egyptian visitors as "Abas" and "Ahmed." Jacques was merely "Jack." The Egyptians were members of the crew of a freighter, the S.S. *Ali Al Bahri,* recently docked in Jersey City, New Jersey. Abas, tall and thin, with dark curly hair, had green eyes and a mechanical smile which he turned on and off like a flashlight whenever he finished speaking. Ahmed, a husky six-footer with black hair and penetrating black eyes, seemed more human, more friendly. He also seemed to be Abas' superior.

Jacques asked if he could get a quantity of heroin like that in the sample that Weasel had delivered. The Egyptians grinned and Ahmed said, "We get you heroin, hashish, opium, cocaine—whatever you want." He stopped smiling. "If you got money," he added.

"How much for the heroin?" Jacques asked.

"Good price," Ahmed said, nodding. "One kilo, eight thousand dollars." A kilo is about two and one-fifth pounds avoirdupois.

"Eight grand!" Jacques exclaimed. "Don't be silly, sailor. You mean six, don't you?"

Ahmed scowled. "Pure stuff, Jack," he said. "Eight grand is bottom price. You take or not?"

"How do I know it's pure stuff?"

George Maskedon spoke. "I'll guarantee it, kid. I been doing business with these guys for years. They handle only good stuff."

"What about prices on other goods?" Jacques asked.

"Sure," Ahmed answered, "whatever you want. Raw opium? One kilo, one grand. Hashish? About a hundred a gram."

"A hundred a gram for tea?"

"Well, for you maybe a little less. Maybe six hundred grams for five hundred bucks."

"Cocaine?" Jacques asked.

Ahmed glanced at Abas. "Very expensive," Abas said, "but we can get."

"You bring any stuff with you on the boat?" Jacques asked.

Ignoring the question, Ahmed stood up. "We got to get back to ship," he said, and then spoke to Abas in Arabic, which Jacques was unable to understand.

"I'll drive you to the dock if you want," Jacques said.

"Not necessary," Ahmed answered.

"It's okay. No trouble."

"Never mind," Ahmed said. "But if you like to drive us to Hudson Tube Terminal, is okay."

On the way to the terminal Jacques noticed with satisfaction that his team of shadowers was still on the job. He spoke to the seamen about making a deal right away if they had anything to sell. "And there's no reason to get Maskedon in on this," he said. "He's just a middleman. You sell me, I pay you, everybody is happy."

In low voices the Egyptians spoke in Arabic, then Ahmed said, "We got about five pounds hashish. You want this?"

They were near the terminal now. Jacques parked the car and invited the pair to have coffee in a nearby restaurant. As they sat at a table, Jacques saw two other agents come in and sit at different tables.

"How much for the hashish?" he asked.

They finally settled on a price of two hundred and fifty dollars for about eleven ounces. "First I'll have to check with my people," Jacques said. He went to a telephone booth and called the Bureau of Narcotics.

"Make a two-hundred-dollar buy," he was told, "and let it go through. We'll try to find their source of supply."

Back at the table the agent said, "My people aren't too much interested in 'tea' right now—they just bought a load from Mexico. But they'll go for two hundred bucks' worth."

The three left the restaurant and drove to Jersey City, where the Egyptians suggested that Jacques wait for them in a nearby tavern while they went to their ship. They returned about 1:30 A.M. and motioned Jacques to come outside, which he did.

"We do business in the car," Ahmed said.

As they sat in the automobile, Abas took a canvas bag from underneath his jacket. "Here's the stuff," he said. "You pay the money."

Jacques made a cursory inspection of the contents of the bag, then handed over two hundred-dollar bills. The three men shook hands and the agent said, "When do you dock here again? We'll be doing more business with each other."

They had a coastwise voyage, they said, and were due in Jersey City again on August 1. Jacques made an appointment to meet them at the tavern near the pier.

On August 1 they kept the appointment and reported to Jacques that they still had about three kilos of hashish which they would sell for eighteen hundred dollars. After some convincing bargaining Jacques succeeded in getting the price down to seventeen hundred dollars, and as instructed he bought all three kilos (which would later be used as evidence).

"Now look," he said, "I don't want any more hashish— at least not for a while. I want other stuff—heroin, opium, cocaine. You going to get some for me?"

Ahmed shrugged. "The price on the white stuff (heroin) has gone up," he said. "Ten grand for one kilo."

"Ten grand! You told me it was eight."

"Yes, but now we hear that the cops got two big outfits —one in Lebanon, one in Marseilles. The supply is cut down, the price goes up." He patted Jacques gently on one arm. "But we do the best we can for you, my friend. You tell Ahmed what you want, eh?" Ahmed brought out a small red leather notebook and a pencil.

"Okay," Jacques said. "You bring one kilo of heroin, two kilos of opium and about ten grams of cocaine."

"Only ten grams?"

"As a sample. I want to see the stuff first. The heroin will be all right if it's like that first sample you had at the old man's house." Jacques glanced at Ahmed's notations written in the notebook in Arabic. "How much for the whole shipment?"

"Who knows?" Ahmed said. "I do the best I can. You pay me just what it costs and a little commission, eh?"

"I can't help myself," Jacques replied, "but I'll tell you something. I have an uncle in Europe who knows the current market prices. He'll tell me what's what, so don't figure on making me a chump—understand?"

Pointing to his notebook Ahmed said, "You better give me address where I can write to you if I have to."

Jacques took the book and wrote the name "Jack Burns" and a Brooklyn address.

The S.S. *Ali Al Bahri* again docked at Jersey City on September 27, when Jacques went to the tavern to meet the Egyptians. There he saw Ahmed with two strangers, introduced as "Ali" and "Hapi," his fellow crew members on the freighter. "Our brother Abas could not come this trip, and we could not fill your order," Ahmed said.

"What? How come? What happened?" Jacques asked.

"There was a big replacement of the crew," Ahmed explained. "We could not trust the new ones."

"You mean you didn't bring anything—not anything at all?"

Ahmed leaned across the table. "Only a hundred grams of heroin," he whispered. "One hundred per cent pure stuff."

Jacques pretended to be exceedingly disturbed. As he himself later wrote in his report, "I reprimanded him not only for failing to deliver, but also for failing to notify me. I explained that this was the main reason I had written my address in his notebook."

Pretending that he did not want to telephone from the tavern, Jacques left and managed to meet his squad leader on the street, who instructed him to buy the heroin.

Back at the tavern he asked Ahmed, "How much for the hundred grams?"

"One grand."

"One grand! You're crazy," Jacques said, making as if to depart. Ahmed held him by the arm. After some whispered discussion Ahmed agreed to sell the heroin for six hundred dollars, and left to go to the ship to get it. He returned to the tavern about seven o'clock and with Jacques went to the latter's car, where Ahmed handed the agent a small package wrapped in brown paper.

"I carried it off the ship in my armpit," he said. "The Customs men were around." (The Customs men, co-operating with the Narcotic agents, had deliberately neglected to search the Egyptian.)

"Are you sure this is a hundred grams?" Jacques said. "It feels like a lot of paper."

Ahmed ripped off the brown wrapping, threw it out of the car window and handed Jacques a cellophane package containing a powdery substance. "Good stuff," Ahmed said.

"One hundred per cent pure." Jacques, satisfied that the package contained heroin, handed over six hundred dollars and the pair separated.

On October 9 Jacques again met Ahmed. "Look here," Jacques told him, "I'm not getting anywhere with you. I've got to get a big shipment, you understand? A big shipment. If I have to, I'll go to Beirut myself to make a deal."

"Fine! Excellent!" Ahmed exclaimed. "I tell you what. My ship docks in Genoa on the way to Beirut. We have connections in Genoa. You meet me there and I fix you up, yes?"

"Yes," Jacques said. Then, "If for any reason I can't make it myself, I'll have my uncle meet you in Genoa. All right?"

"All right," Ahmed said. "But how will I know your uncle?"

Jacques took a one-dollar bill from his pocket and handed it to the Egyptian. "You write something on that," he said.

Ahmed wrote some characters in Arabic, then Jacques tore the bill in half and gave one piece to Ahmed. "If I can't make the trip myself, I'll give this half to my uncle. If he meets you in Genoa, don't talk with him unless he has the half of the bill to match your half."

Agent Jacques's half of the bill was promptly forwarded to Narcotic Agent James Bible, stationed in Europe, with an account of developments in the case to date. Jacques also wrote to Ahmed, saying that he would be represented by his uncle. On November 17 Bible met the S.S. *Ali Al Bahri* when it docked at Genoa, and a mess boy showed him where he could find Ahmed.

As Bible approached, Ahmed put out his hand and said cordially, "I know who you are!" After comparing the matching halves of the dollar bill, Ahmed presented Bible with a package of English cigarettes and arranged to meet him at the Hotel Plaza that afternoon.

Ahmed called at the hotel about one o'clock with a friend he introduced as "Mr. Moustaches," another seaman

from the freighter. Mr. Moustaches explained that he was
Ahmed's boss and had been selling narcotics in New York
for some six years, but had never met the "nephew" Jacques.
Apparently Mr. Moustaches considered Bible trustworthy,
for he answered his questions without hesitation.

"We bring hashish and opium to Genoa and Marseilles,"
he said, "and there we pick up heroin which we sell in the
United States. Very simple."

"That's what my nephew wants—heroin," Bible said.
"Can you fix us up?"

Mr. Moustaches laughed. "I can send you to a connection
in Marseilles who makes ninety-five per cent pure stuff.
All you want."

"Fine! Who is it? Where do I find this connection?"

Mr. Moustaches got up to leave. "Tomorrow," he said, "I
give you a letter of introduction. All right?"

"Very good," Bible said.

The next day, as promised, Mr. Moustaches came to the
hotel and gave Bible a note to a French perfume dealer in
Marseilles. Written in French on one side of the paper was
the message, "M. Maurice: I come recommended by Ahmed
of the S.S. *Ali Al Bahri.*" On the other side the note read,
"Dear Maurice: I send with the bearer the sum of twenty
thousand francs, balance due from last time. Please let him
pass and give him anything he wants for cash." The signature was illegible.

Mr. Moustaches gave Bible twenty thousand francs to
deliver to M. Maurice in Marseilles.

A few days later Bible, working with French authorities,
checked in at a Marseilles hotel and wasted no time in
heading for the perfume establishment of M. Maurice.
Maurice was in his office and Bible handed him the note
and money.

Maurice, tall and dark, with sharp eyes and a shrewd
manner, read the note and juggled the money in one hand.

"I am sorry, monsieur," he said, "but there is some mistake. I am not acquainted with anyone named Ahmed, I do not know this ship, and I am not entitled to this money." He laughed. "I wish I were."

"You are M. Maurice, are you not?" Bible asked.

"I am."

"Is there any other Maurice at this address?"

"But no—I am the only one." He shook his head. "It is strange, very strange."

"Perhaps one of your friends or employees has been selling perfume to seamen and has used your name?"

Maurice nodded thoughtfully. "This is possible. I shall inquire. You come back tomorrow."

The following morning Bible visited Maurice again, and this time Maurice introduced him to a pale, skinny man named Barone, who wanted to know how Bible knew Mr. Moustaches and Ahmed.

"I've been doing business with them for years," Bible said. "If their ship had come to Marseilles they would have brought me to you."

Barone explained that he had sold them perfume and that they believed him to be Maurice. They owed him the twenty thousand francs. "Now," Barone said, "what is it you want?"

Bible said that he wanted at least half a kilo of heroin.

"We don't like to sell less than a kilo," Barone said. They dickered back and forth, with Barone finally agreeing to sell Bible half a kilo for about thirteen hundred dollars.

The next day, when delivery was to be made, Barone announced that the deal was off. "My boss thinks you might be a cop," he said. "He thinks we were tailed by some strangers yesterday. He wants to wait until the ship comes to Marseilles so he can talk with our mutual friends."

"You tell your boss he's crazy," Bible said. "If I were a

cop I could have locked up our sailor friends long before this."

"I'm sorry," Barone answered. "I'd like to do business with you, but—well, the boss is getting old and suspicious. He doesn't like to take chances. We'll have to wait until the ship docks in Marseilles."

"Let me talk to the boss. Maybe I can change his mind."

Barone laughed. "I told you—he thinks you're a cop. He'd never talk to you—not even to say hello."

About five weeks later Bible went to Genoa, where he met Ahmed, Moustaches and another seaman named Serge. Serge, it developed, had written the note of introduction to Maurice, from whom he had bought narcotics for years. Ahmed, Moustaches and Serge were partners—Serge buying the drugs, the other two distributing them. He would be glad, Serge said, to vouch for Bible to Maurice.

The freighter docked in Marseilles on January 28, 1958, when Bible met Moustaches and Serge and went to Maurice's establishment. Maurice was not in, but they went to a bar next door where they saw Barone.

"What's the matter with you?" Serge asked. "You won't do business with our friend? We have been dealing with him for five years, at least. If you can't trust him, you can't trust anybody."

Barone suddenly stood up and walked away hurriedly.

He returned in half an hour. "Did you see them?" he asked. "While we were talking, three detectives from the Police Narcotic Squad came to the bar." He scowled at Bible. "Maybe the boss is right about you."

Serge took Barone aside and whispered to him. They returned to the table and Serge said, "Barone has a proposition. He will deliver a kilo of heroin in one hour. You pay him without opening the package."

Bible smiled slyly. "What do you take me for?" he said.

"I'm not paying out two or three grand for a package of sugar. I want to see what I'm getting." He glared at Barone. "Look here, I'm fed up with your attitude. It's costing me money to run around from here to Genoa and Paris, all for nothing. You wanted a personal introduction from our friends. You've had it. If you want to do business, I'll be at my hotel. If not, forget it."

Barone apparently chose—or was ordered—to forget it, for he made no further attempts to negotiate with Bible. Arrangements were made, however, for Ahmed and Serge to take a "shipment" to America for sale to their friend Jack.

On February 9 the S.S. *Ali Al Bahri* docked in Jersey City, where Jacques met Ahmed, Abas, Moustaches and Serge, who told him what had transpired in Marseilles (which Bible had already reported). They said they had brought Jacques a full kilo of heroin and would deliver it the following day.

On February 10 Jacques met Moustaches in Jersey City and they drove to the Hudson Tube, where they found Ahmed standing near the entrance, holding a "camel saddle" hassock—a cushion on a wooden crosspiece between two X-shaped ends.

"Have you got the stuff?" Jacques asked.

Ahmed pointed to the hassock and suggested that they talk in the car. Moustaches left, saying he was going back to the ship. In the car Ahmed separated the cushion from the saddle, unlaced the bottom of the cushion and extracted two roll-shaped newspaper packages. Opening one, Jacques saw a powdery substance.

"It doesn't look very good," he said.

"It's one hundred per cent pure stuff," Ahmed answered.

"I want a better look at it," Jacques said. "You wait here."

He went into the lavatory at the near-by tavern, where

his closer examination convinced him that the package contained a harmless nonnarcotic powder. He returned to the car.

"This is no good," he said.

"What do you mean, no good? It's a hundred per cent pure!" Ahmed insisted.

"A hundred per cent of nothing," Jacques said. "We're going to get Serge. He's the guy who negotiated this deal in Marseilles."

They met Serge at the tavern bar. "This I do not understand," he said, when told that it was not heroin. "Ahmed and Moustaches and I made the deal with Maurice in Marseilles. It's the same stuff as the samples you got before."

As they prepared to leave the bar, Jacques signaled other Narcotic agents and when Jacques, Ahmed and Serge were about to enter Jacques's car, all three were placed under arrest and taken to the pier where the freighter was docked. There they found Moustaches in the custody of another group of agents. With the help of Customs inspectors the entire ship was searched from stem to stern, but without result.

On the basis of the sale of hashish and heroin, and the conspiracy to sell narcotics, Ahmed, Abas, Serge and Moustaches were sentenced in a federal court in Newark, New Jersey, to serve five years in a federal penitentiary.

"The old man," George Maskedon, died on December 2, 1957. The Weasel was not prosecuted because of his assistance to the agents.

Thanks to the co-operating French police in Marseille, Barone was arrested there, but was later released by a French court order.

M. Maurice was not arrested, since there was not enough direct evidence to link him to the narcotic traffic. It appears that he was "the boss" and that his suspicion of Agent Bible was so strong that he and Barone delivered the harmless powder to their trusted seamen friends in the hope that if they *were* dealing with undercover agents, the evidence would not be incriminating.

This, then, has been a true account of a typical undercover case developed by the Bureau of Narcotics. Many of these cases are dramatic, even violent, and some Narcotic agents have sacrificed their lives in their fight against the drug evil. These, however, are the exception rather than the rule.

Because opium, heroin, marijuana and other illicit drugs are smuggled into the United States by land, sea or air, the Bureau of Narcotics works closely with the Treasury enforcement agency that has been the nemesis of smugglers since the days of George Washington—the Bureau of Customs. Behind the scenes the Customs agents have devised ways to detect some of the ingenious methods used by smugglers. This explains the reasons why they find it so difficult to sneak contraband past the most alert eyes in the world.

9

CHALLENGE TO THE CHEAT

Passengers walked down the gangplank waving at friends on the pier, grinning with it's good-to-be-home-again greetings. Shouts blended with the rumble of trucks and the hollow toots of auto horns, and the smell of burning gasoline was in the air. A dark man, a hunchback, neatly dressed in a blue suit and black Homburg, reached the end of the gangplank and tried to hurry. He stumbled and fell, and a young Customs inspector rushed to help him to his feet.

The dark man pulled away from the inspector's grip and said nervously, "Thank you. Pretty clumsy of me, wasn't it? Thank you very much." He started away, but the inspector stopped him.

"Excuse me, sir," he said politely, "but would you mind coming with me for a few moments?"

The hunchback paled. "I'm all right, Officer, quite all right, I assure you. And I really am in a hurry." He turned quickly. The inspector grabbed his wrist.

"I'll have to insist," he said.

"But why? What's it all about? Just because I fell down—"

"Will you come along, please? You'll find out soon enough."

It was the inspector who had found out. His hand on the hunched back had felt something unlike flesh, something softer. When the "hunchback" was searched, Customs men found his "hump" to be a cache of jewelry—rings, pendants, pins, necklaces. All were wrapped in a large wad of cotton held tightly against the man's back by three medicinal plasters, an ingenious smuggling scheme which might have succeeded if a Customs officer had not performed a good deed.

The smuggler confessed that he had made twenty-seven transatlantic trips and that once, when he had brought his brother's body to America for burial, he had smuggled in forty-three rings by putting them on the partly concealed fingers of the corpse! Like many other criminals, he sought to avoid the payment of duties which make up an important part of the national revenue collected by the Bureau of Customs.

The collection of customs as revenue dates from ancient times. The New Testament says that Jesus called Matthew from "the receipt of customs," indicating that Matthew was a customs collector at the Sea of Galilee. The term "customs" was used centuries ago when feudal barons were privileged to levy taxes, especially upon imported merchandise or for selling various domestic commodities. Merchants entering different provinces, expecting to pay these taxes, would ask, "What are the customs?" meaning, "How much tribute do you exact if I take my goods into your land?"

The word "tariff" has an equally interesting origin. Born of plunder and death, it comes from the town of Tarifa on the Spanish coast near Gibraltar. Situated on a high cliff and connected with the coast by a narrow causeway, Tarifa was founded centuries ago by the Moors and later used as headquarters by a gang of thieves who held up merchant ships and exacted tribute on all cargoes according to a fixed scale, so that mariners soon referred to payments "for Tarifa," or tariff.

Our tariff laws are very complicated, and in at least one case the government lost considerable money because of a tiny typographical error. This became known as "The Comma Case" because in writing the Tariff Act of June 6, 1872, a clerk changed a hyphen to a comma in a paragraph dealing with the importation of fruit and plants. The wording, "tropical fruit, plants, etc.," should have read "tropical fruit-plants, etc." Because of the error, tropical fruit was imported free of duty, although it was intended that only fruit *plants* should be on the free list. The punctuation error cost Uncle Sam about three million dollars before Congress corrected the language to require duty on fruit.

Names of some famous Americans have appeared on the Customs pay roll, including that of President Chester A. Arthur, who was Collector of Customs for the port of New York. Nathaniel Hawthorne (author of *The Scarlet Letter*) was a "measurer" at the Boston Customhouse at a salary of fifteen hundred dollars a year. Edwin Arlington Robinson, famous poet (*The Man Against the Sky*, etc.), was a Customs employee in New York, and Herman Melville of *Moby Dick* fame was a Customs inspector in New York during his last years.

Does the work of the Customs Bureau affect you and me? It certainly does. The clay used in making the dishes in your kitchen may have crossed the sea from England. The cane fields of Cuba probably produced the sugar you use with your food. The paper on which the morning news is printed probably came across the border from Canada. The tin in cans or other containers on our shelves may have come from Bolivia, the Malay States or the Dutch East Indies. If your hi-fi record player has a diamond needle, the diamond may have been mined in South Africa. Your linen handkerchiefs may have been imported from Ireland. The lens on your camera may have come from Germany, Japan or some other foreign land. All of these—and more—must clear through Customs.

Take a look at the ships in our harbors. There are big ships and small ones, grimy ones and bright ones, with names on their bows from the ends of the earth. All these are part of our bustling Customs life, a part of our important role in the ceaseless flow of people and goods arriving at the United States frontiers.

In a typical peacetime year, from thirty-five to forty million vessels, aircraft, automobiles, busses, trains and other carriers cross our borders or enter our harbors, bringing in more than one hundred million passengers carrying some twenty-five million pieces of baggage. In addition, some twenty-five million pedestrians walk across our international boundaries.

The Bureau of Customs is responsible for inspecting this multitude of carriers and people. The bureau also controls Customs warehousing of imported goods and determines the amount of "drawback"—Customs duties to be refunded on goods imported from one country to be exported to another. It keeps a constant vigil against frauds on the Customs revenue, and quick hands are ready to nab violators of the Customs laws. It is, in short, our challenge to the cheat.

The smuggler is a cheat who generally cheats himself, for he will be caught sooner or later. Smugglers are not always the swarthy villains pictured in movies and television dramas, nor are they always suave gentlemen or sophisticated ladies. They are composites of these and ordinary people—some hardened criminals, some merely adventurous experimenters. And they don't smuggle only jewels and drugs. Liquor, tobacco, furs, wool and silks are high on the list—even food, if and when a shortage creates a good market.

When wartime food rationing was in effect, a Customs agent unearthed information that food was being sneaked across the border from Canada. With other officers the agent spied on the purchase of meat and butter by a railroad conductor, a train cook and a brakeman at a Montreal butcher shop. The trio was shadowed to a waiting train in Montreal and to St. Albans, Vermont, where the Customs men seized several hams, sides of beef, lamb, pork and more than fifty pounds of butter, all cleverly hidden in various parts of the train, all intended to be sold at high prices. The smugglers were arrested.

One of the most exciting captures in Customs Bureau annals was made a few years ago when Customs and Narcotic agents triumphed in a thrilling gun duel with Mexican drug runners near Calexico, California. Mastermind of the ring was José Remora, bank robber, killer, gang boss of Lower California. His close adviser was another unsavory character known widely as "The Professor."

Narcotic Agent John Wilson, working under cover, was able to complete a deal with this pair for delivery of one hundred and thirty-nine cans of smoking opium. Remora insisted that the delivery be made in a specified area along the All-American Canal, seven miles west of Calexico.

Agent Wilson agreed to this location, although he was well aware of the reasons why this particular spot had been chosen by the smuggler. "This area," Wilson reported to his superiors, "is flat farming country about one and a half miles from Highway 98. A dirt road extends the length of the canal and parallels a dirt road about fifty feet north of the canal. Between these two roads is a culvert filled with low underbrush. The canal road and the country road parallel to it are connected by a dirt road about fifty feet long which is in direct line with the Woodbine Check Bridge that crosses the canal into Mexican territory. Because of the geography it is impossible for any men to enter the vicinity prior to the meeting time, in order to conceal themselves. An automobile or men on foot could readily be seen from the banks of the canal. Therefore, as many officers as possible must conceal themselves in the agent's automobile and drive to the meeting place at the appointed time."

In line with this plan a Customs officer hid in the trunk of Wilson's car. The cushion of the rear seat was removed and two other Customs officers and a Narcotic agent lay on the car floor covered by a blanket on which were placed several empty suitcases. Two more Customs men sped to a ranch house about half a mile from the rendezvous, where they could watch the bridge with binoculars and be prepared to halt the flight of any smugglers.

Wilson's car was a veritable arsenal on wheels. In addition to the revolver carried by each man, the car carried four riot guns and a 30/30 carbine. When everything was set, at dusk Wilson drove the car to the meeting place at the canal.

Standing near the bridge were four Mexicans, each with an automatic pistol strapped to his waist. Wilson stopped the car about fifty paces from the four and got out. Two of the Mexicans left the group, carrying a burlap sack containing the opium. The two proved to be Remora himself and one of his lieutenants called Pablo. The third Mexican, gaily dressed in a light yellow silk sport shirt, tan slacks, and a Panama hat, followed the pair with the sack. The fourth man stayed at the bridge. The trio met Wilson close to the car and stopped.

"Here's the stuff," Remora said, putting the sack down.

"I want to look at it," Wilson said.

"Okay, go ahead."

Wilson opened the sack and inspected the cans of opium.

"All right. The money's in the trunk of the car. I'll get it."

This was the signal, and the men concealed in the car prepared to move fast.

Wilson went to the trunk, Remora and his two cohorts at his elbow. The agent raised the lid and the Customs man leaped out. Instantly the three Mexicans grabbed their automatics and began to shoot. Wilson and the Customs man ducked behind the car, their own guns roaring.

Now the car doors flew open and the three officers hidden in the rear seat came out blazing away. Suddenly a volley of rifle fire thundered from the underbrush in the culvert, where Remora had concealed a squad of his killers.

A bullet from Wilson's revolver plowed into the belly of the fourth Mexican in Remora's original group. As he whirled around, two more zipped through his back and he fell into the underbrush. Some of the agents plunged into the culvert for cover; others kept close to the car. Remora fled into the darkness, firing as he went. Pursuit would have been fatal, since rifle and pistol bullets whammed into the car and screamed past the culvert which protected the agents. Pablo, also trying to flee, stumbled and dropped his gun. He lay still and made no attempt to move. He was holding the sack with the opium.

Now the Customs men who had been posted at the ranch house arrived and opened fire on the Mexicans. A rifle cracked at the bridge, where a Mexican tried to pick off the agents in the culvert. A Customs man took careful aim at the sniper, fired once, saw him spin around, fall, then crawl away into Mexican territory.

The gun battle raged for nearly an hour before the Mexicans ceased fire. The agents, none of whom was wounded, pounced on Pablo and the one hundred and thirty-nine cans of opium. The Mexican who was shot and who fell into the brush had apparently crawled away and escaped. The others had vanished in the darkness. With their prisoner and contraband the agents withdrew in Wilson's car, now riddled with jagged bullet holes.

Remora became a fugitive, but his Number One boy—"The Professor"—was captured by Customs officers when he ventured across the border a month after the shooting. He was sent to the penitentiary for ten years. Ironically, Pablo, Remora's lieutenant, was acquitted by a jury which believed his unlikely story that he had been forced under threat of death to accompany the smugglers.

Besides drugs, smugglers believe there is profit in expensive foreign watch movements—if they could just get past Customs. Not long ago a clergyman was caught in New York with twelve hundred watch movements hidden next to his skin in a specially made cloth vest. One enterprising American in Switzerland bought several hundred movements in the firm conviction that he had invented a foolproof idea to get them into the United States duty free. Since they were very thin, he folded nine or ten in a piece of cardboard, padding them firmly with paper. Then he put the cardboard into a heavy plain envelope, which thus appeared to contain merely a bulky letter. Filling twenty such envelopes, he addressed them in different names to various hotels along the Atlantic seaboard and shipped them as first-class mail, which would ordinarily be delivered unopened. However, in the upper left-hand corners he rubber-stamped a very faint impression: *"May be opened for Customs inspection; invoice enclosed."* In other words, he was smuggling by pretending to comply with the Customs laws.

An alert Customs inspector in Baltimore, Maryland, noticed the ghostlike impression on one of the letters, opened it and found the watch movements but no invoice. Customs agents launched an investigation which trapped the sender in Switzerland and his accomplices in the United States, winning another game of hide-and-seek.

Finding Customs-proof hiding places is one of the smuggler's greatest problems because, to a Customs inspector, practically every object is capable of holding contraband. One smuggler cut out the centers of all the pages in a Zane Grey novel, *The Shepherd of Guadalupe,* and filled the opening with narcotics. The Customs men read him like a book!

An importer prepared to pay duty on a shipment of toy roulette games, each about two inches square. The wary Customs men took apart one of the games, revealing a costly "toy"—a neatly-concealed, high-priced Swiss watch movement. A variation of this device was a shipment of one-and-one-half-inch brass gear wheels, each ingeniously made of two pieces fastened together to cover a watchworks.

Some smugglers try the "big time," like the two women who flew into New York from Europe and alighted from their plane carrying two identical suitcases. The Customs inspectors, searching the bags, found $270,000 worth of unset diamonds! Each suitcase was braced inside with a steel strip about two inches wide and half an inch thick. Pockets had been drilled in the steel to carry the gems. Some slots which held no jewels contained tissue paper bearing faint impressions of $20 gold coins, indicating that gold had been smuggled out of the country, diamonds in.

Gold coin worth $135,150 was seized in one case in Brooklyn, New York, because a Customs inspector questioned the weight of an automobile being shipped to Rotterdam. The car tipped the scales at 3600 pounds, whereas the inspector owned one just like it, weighing only 3200 pounds. He began a search. In a compartment hollowed out under the rear seat he found the extra 400 pounds—2550 gleaming 50-peso Mexican gold coins.

One man even tried to smuggle gold out of the country by manufacturing a complete automobile fender of solid

gold, painted to match the rest of his car. Here again the
weight gave away the scheme and the smuggler went to
jail.

False-bottom luggage and the hollowed heels and soles
of shoes are ancient hiding places. More ingenious, but no
safer, are the craws of parrots or other birds, the seed dishes
in canary cages, hollow bracelets, cigars, cigarettes and
flowers. One apparently respectable botanist made trips
regularly to and from South America to get orchid specimens and bulbs. Suspecting him of smuggling, Customs
agents made a search which was fruitless until they discovered almost-invisible scars on some bulbs of *Orchis Odon-
toglossoms,* a common variety. Cut open, the scarred bulbs
sprouted a fortune in diamonds.

Flowers and other plants from abroad must pass Customs
scrutiny under Department of Agriculture quarantine regu-
lations, designed to keep plant diseases and pests from
harming crops in the United States. Animals, too, are held
up by Customs until passed by the Bureau of Animal Industry, for they may be unwitting smugglers of disease and
death.

To the Customs Bureau the smuggling of goods out of
the country is as important as smuggling them in. One problem has been the attempts to smuggle arms, ammunition and
implements of war out of the United States to rebels in
other countries for use in battling existing governments, in
violation of the Mutual Security Act. While this law is administered by our Department of State, it is enforced on our
coasts and borders by the Bureau of Customs.

In 1958, Mr. Ralph Kelly, Commissioner of Customs, told
a Congressional Committee that on November 8, 1957, a
Customs agent at Miami, Florida, received information that
Cuban rebels had bought the vessel *Philomar III* to use in
transporting thirty-five "fully equipped men" and a quantity
of arms and military supplies to Cuba.

"The vessel," said Commissioner Kelly, "was kept under constant surveillance by the United States Immigration Patrol until she sailed from Tampa. She was later located at Piney Point, Big Pine Key, Florida, where she was carefully watched by Customs agents and inspectors, assisted by Alcohol and Tobacco Tax agents and other government officers. During this time merchandise was observed being taken from a car and laden on the craft. On the night of November 8 the officers converged on the vessel. A search revealed a Thompson submachine gun, a Garand rifle, and an antitank rifle. During the night six additional automobiles arrived on the scene with men, arms, ammunition and implements of war destined for Cuba and intended to be placed on the vessel. A total of thirty-one offenders were arrested, and the vessel, seven automobiles, and the arms, ammunition, implements of war and other equipment in considerable quantity were seized by the officers."

Smuggling is something almost everyone thinks he could do if he tried. Like writing or acting, it looks easy and appears to be profitable. Detection seems unlikely. So attractive is this reasoning that, according to Customs records, one out of every five tourists is a potential smuggler. Smuggling is not always deliberate, however. Sometimes travelers unfamiliar with Customs laws and declarations may innocently overlook certain items in their possession. The nature of the merchandise and character of the individual in each case helps to determine whether there will be a penalty or merely a correction in the declaration and payment of duty, if any is required. When in doubt, always ask the Customs man.

Briefly, if you are a resident of the United States returning to this country from abroad, you must declare in writing *everything* you acquired in another country. Members of a family living in one household and traveling together may file a single declaration—a simple form which generally requires only a few "yes" or "no" answers.

You will be required to list articles which (1) you are bringing home for someone else at that person's request, (2) you intend to sell or use in your business, (3) do not accompany you on your return (that is, those which are being sent to you from abroad at your request), and (4) liquor and cigars if they exceed the quantities permitted under exemptions.

Every traveler who acquires articles for personal or household use and who properly declares them, is entitled to free entry up to the value of two hundred, three hundred or even five hundred dollars, depending upon the circumstances. If you ordered the articles *before* you left the United States, the exemptions do not apply, nor do they apply to gifts you send from abroad to friends or relatives.

The two-hundred-dollar exemption usually applies only when you have been outside the country for at least forty-eight hours on the trip from which you are returning, although there is no time restriction for articles acquired in Mexico if you return through a port in Texas, Arizona or New Mexico. This two-hundred-dollar exemption, however, is not allowable more often than once in any thirty-one-day period.

The three-hundred-dollar exemption is in addition to the one for two hundred dollars, but you can get it only if you have been abroad at least twelve full days and have not claimed the exemption within six months prior to your return from this trip. If, within three years, you should sell any article passed free under this exemption, the article is subject to forfeiture unless full duty is paid on it before it is sold.

Not more than one gallon of an alcoholic beverage, nor more than one hundred cigars may be brought in without payment of duty under the exemption. More may be brought in, but will be subject to duties and taxes. Also, Customs officers will not release liquors destined to any state for use in violation of the laws of that state.

The value of articles for Customs purposes is based upon fair market value. In making either an oral or written declaration, tell the Customs officer how much you paid for your merchandise. Don't guess and don't try to cheat—he knows more about values than you realize. If you acquired any article by gift, tell the Customs man what you consider a fair market value.

Evaluation of imported merchandise and determination of its components by the Customs Bureau is essential to the fair assessment of Customs duties. Years ago a Customs examiner in a small port inspected the original statue of the "Venus de Milo," sent to this country for an exhibition. He marked it "NCV" (No Commercial Value)—"Arms broken." Today, however, practically all Customs examiners are experts, and several Customs laboratories are maintained to test samples of sugar, wool, metals and other merchandise.

Not every pound of cargo is tested, of course, but one official explains that "the importers never know which part of a shipment we will test. In the case of wool, the duties paid on the basis of our laboratory tests will run about two per cent higher than the duties resulting from the visual test, so there is no question but what our laboratories more than pay for themselves. Also," he adds, "importers are in favor of the laboratory because, for the first time, the horse-trading element has been taken out of the paying of duties on wool and every importer stands on the same basis. There is no fear that some competitors are getting an unfair advantage at the Customhouse. The laboratory test is much more accurate than the feel-smell-and-look test which is the traditional method of the twenty-five-thousand-dollar-a-year commercial expert."

Other experts who "see and tell" are responsible for swelling the Customs coffers on the one hand and depleting them on the other. They are the professional and amateur informers who may lawfully collect twenty-five per cent of any recovery for furnishing original information leading to that recovery. The percentage and the conditions governing its payment are fixed by the Tariff Act of 1930, which sets a ceiling of fifty thousand dollars for any single payment. In 1936 the Treasury paid the full fifty thousand dollars in each of two cases for original information which resulted in the collection of three million dollars in Customs duties and taxes from certain foreign distilleries and their associates. This maximum has been paid in few other cases, and the average yearly rewards to informers *total* perhaps fifty thousand dollars.

Informers are often disgruntled former employees, like the maid who exposed a plot by certain famous American entertainers to smuggle jewelry into the United States some time ago. Others who reveal smuggling schemes may be envious acquaintances or personal enemies of would-be smugglers, professionals interested only in the rewards, or good citizens inspired by patriotic motives. Once their information is reported, the Customs Bureau alerts its inspectors and agents.

The men who inspect baggage at our docks and borders are Customs inspectors. Those who make investigations of real or suspected smugglers are agents of the Bureau's Customs Agency Service, headed by Chester A. Emerick, a career enforcement officer. They all work closely with their brother investigators in the Bureau of Narcotics and other Treasury enforcement agencies.

How do they work? Well, here is a typical Customs case involving an attempt to sneak a rather large quantity of marijuana across the Mexican border into the United States.

10

CAPTURE

At exactly three o'clock on a bright April afternoon, young Juan Perfidio stopped his six-year-old Buick sedan at the Customs Inspection Station on the United States side of the International Bridge at Laredo, Texas.

Customs inspectors Martin and Cistrano asked the usual questions, including, "Have you anything to declare?"

"Only two bottles of liquor and some carved wood curios," Juan said, showing them.

"Get out, please," Inspector Martin said. "We'll look the car over."

Quickly Juan said, "But no—I mean—I have told you what I am bringing in."

"Get out, please," Inspector Martin said again.

Juan got out, moving his arms nervously and muttering in Spanish. The inspectors glanced at each other and Inspector Cistrano said, "You'd better come along with us, boy."

"Where to?" Juan asked.

"Just to the Search Room."

As they walked toward the Customs Building, Juan began to chatter excitedly, insisting that no personal search was necessary and that the inspectors would find no contraband. He was, he said, an upholsterer by trade, and had left his home in Chicago three weeks before to go—alone—to Mexico City on a pleasure trip. What was wrong with that?

Nothing, the Customs men decided. Although they found no contraband on his person, Juan was so jittery that they were sure he was hiding something. They returned to the car with him.

"Lift up the hood," Inspector Martin ordered.

"The hood? Oh—well, I have to go around to the right side. The—the hood won't open from the left."

"That so?" Inspector Cistrano said. Snapping open the hood fasteners he lifted the hood from the left side without difficulty. "Seems all right to me." He leaned over the motor, and in the air vent on the left side he saw a plastic bag. He glanced at Inspector Martin. "Well, well," he said. "Look here, will you?"

Inspector Cistrano straightened up and walked over to Juan. Without warning Juan shoved him backward, turned, then ran around the car. Inspector Martin sped after him. Suddenly Juan stopped and wheeled, striking Martin in the face and stomach. As the inspector tumbled to the pavement, Juan rushed along the road leading into Laredo.

Other Customs officers and a few bystanders, seeing the attack on the inspectors, joined in the chase. Juan, confused and panic stricken, dashed into the back yard of a private home—a yard surrounded by a high fence. As he tried frantically to climb over it, he was grabbed by the Assistant Supervisory Customs Inspector, one of his pursuers. They struggled for a few moments, but the Customs man, trained to cope with just such an opponent, was able to bring Juan's right arm behind his back in a secure hammer lock, immobilizing him. He was brought back to the Customs

Inspection Station and handcuffed, and the inspectors then notified the Customs agents in Laredo.

In response to the call, Customs agents George Lamar and Ricardo Dioso hurried to the International Bridge to question Juan Perfidio. At the bridge they found the inspectors searching Juan's car as the handcuffed prisoner looked on.

From underneath the chassis the inspectors unscrewed some metal plates which had been bolted to the body, and as the plates came away several large plastic bags fell to the roadway. The Customs men opened the sacks—they were filled with prepared marijuana.

"Well, now, Juan," Lamar said, "I wonder how all that marijuana got under there, and just who owns it. Do you happen to know?"

Juan looked at the packages for a long moment, then shrugged in a gesture of defeat. "It's mine," he said. "I put it there." Quickly he added, "But it was an accident! I didn't mean to get mixed up in anything like this when I left Chicago."

"An accident?" Lamar asked. "How could it be an accident? It seems to me it was pretty well planned."

"I mean it was an accident the way I got it in the first place."

"Tell us about it," Dioso suggested.

"Well," Juan said, "about three hundred miles north of Mexico City I pulled off the road to rest a few minutes. You know—I didn't want to doze off while I was driving. Down the road I saw a big truck unload some boxes in the ditch and drive away. I was out in open country, and I couldn't figure why they would want to leave any boxes there. At first I thought the boxes might be empty, but then I drove down and opened them—and they were filled with this stuff." He pointed at the seized packages. "I knew what it was."

"Were there any markings on the boxes?" Lamar asked.

"No. No markings. I looked for some myself."

"Any name on the truck?"

"I couldn't see any."

"All right. You found the boxes. Then what?"

"I figured maybe I could make some money if I could sell the stuff, so I loaded the boxes into my car and drove to Mexico City. I went to a hotel and took the marijuana out of the boxes and packed it in these sacks. I bought the metal sheets and bolted them underneath the car, the way you found them."

"Just where did you intend to sell the stuff?" Dioso asked.

"Oh, I was going to take it back to Chicago and try to sell it there."

"To whom?"

"To whom? To anybody. I thought maybe I could find a customer."

"Of course you didn't have anyone in particular in mind?" Dioso said.

"No."

"Have you ever been arrested before?" Lamar asked.

Nodding, Juan answered, "I did six months in the Cook County Jail back in 1944."

"For what?"

"Stealing a car."

"Any other offenses?"

"Well, I got picked up in New York in 1951—or it could have been 1952—for check forgery, but it was a bum rap and I beat it."

"What hotel did you stay at in Mexico City?"

"The Hotel Canada."

A search of Juan's clothing revealed receipts for the purchase of plastic bags from a firm in Mexico City, a photograph of Juan and another man with two scantily dressed women in a night club, and a bill from the Hotel Canada—

but the bill bore the name of Francisco Garcia along with that of Juan Perfidio.

"Who's Francisco Garcia?" he was asked.

He stared at the hotel bill, then turned his hands palms up. "Never heard of him," he said.

"Who are the other people with you in this picture?" Lamar asked.

Juan glanced at the photograph. "I don't know. Just somebody I met in that club. The girls work there."

Juan was lodged in jail in Laredo. At five o'clock in the afternoon Lamar received a telephone call from Customs Inspector Harry Short.

"We just stopped a woman who came from Mexico in a taxicab," Short reported. "She was searched by an inspectress, but we didn't find anything incriminating. I thought I'd better call you, though, because on the inside flap of her purse we found the license number of a car, scribbled in pencil. It's the license number of the Buick driven by that guy who had the load of marijuana."

"We'll be right down," Lamar said. "Hold the woman and the taxi driver."

At the International Bridge, Lamar and Dioso questioned José Perez, the taxi driver, who said that his woman passenger had been put into the cab at the Hotel Flores in Nuevo Laredo, Mexico, by a man with whom she seemed to be quarreling. (Nuevo Laredo, Mexico, adjoins Laredo, Texas.)

Lamar showed Perez the photograph of Juan and his friends in the night club. "Was it one of those men?"

Perez' face brightened and he pointed at Juan's companion. "That's him! That's the man who put her in my cab."

The woman was escorted to the Customs Agency Service office by Lamar and Dioso. Her name, she said, was Lolita Moreno, though she also used the name Rosita Garcia, since Garcia was the name of a husband from whom she was divorced.

"His name is Francisco Garcia?" Dioso asked.

"*Sí*, it is Francisco. You know him?"

"Where is he now?"

She laughed. "Who knows? Chicago, New York, Mexico City. I don't know."

Lamar showed her the license number written on the inside of her purse flap. "What's this number for?" he asked.

She stared at it as though seeing it for the first time. "I never see this before," she answered. "Who put that there?"

Dioso slapped the top of the desk. "I'll tell you who put it there!" he said. "You did."

"But I—"

"You went to Mexico City with your ex-husband and his friend Juan Perfidio to make a deal for marijuana. Your ex-husband was afraid the stuff would be found in Juan's car and he didn't want you riding in it, so he sent you back to the States in a taxicab. But you wrote down the number of Juan's car so you'd be sure to find the right one if it got across the border safely. Isn't that the real story, Lolita?" He threw the picture of Juan and Francisco on the desk. "Look," he said. "You know them, don't you?"

Lolita took one look at the picture, then picked it up and looked more closely. Scowling, she hurled the photograph across the desk. "So that is what he was doing!" she cried. "That was the business deal he told me about!" Breathing heavily, she faced Lamar. "I tell you the truth! I go from Chicago to Mexico City with Juan in his Buick car, and we go to Nuevo Laredo and meet Francisco, my ex-husband." She stopped.

"All right," Lamar said. "What then?"

"Then we—then we—" She stopped again.

"You what?"

"Nothing," she said. "Juan and Francisco had some business to do, and they left me at the hotel. When it was time to go back to the States, Francisco put me in a taxicab. He didn't want me to ride with Juan."

"Why not?" Dioso asked.

"How do I know why not? Maybe he was jealous or something."

"Maybe he didn't want you to get arrested if Juan didn't make it across the border, huh?"

She looked up at Dioso. "Maybe that was the reason. I don't know. Anyway, I didn't know Juan was smuggling anything."

Lamar sighed. "Lolita—I thought you were going to tell us the truth?"

"That is the truth! I swear it! I have told you everything."

"All right," Lamar said. "You'll have some time to think more about it in jail. Come on, lady."

After Lolita was lodged in the county jail to await a hearing, the Customs agents went to the Hotel Flores in Nuevo Laredo, Mexico, and talked with the hotel clerk. He remembered that Francisco and Lolita Garcia had registered as husband and wife, and that they were in the company of a tall, very dark man (Juan Perfidio was tall and very dark). He identified the men from the night club photograph. They had two automobiles, he said—one was a Buick, but he could not remember the make of the other.

On the street near the hotel the agents talked again with Perez, the taxi driver who had driven Lolita to the border. He remembered that the two suspects had hired a boy to wash two automobiles for them, and he later brought the boy to the Customs agents.

"*Si, señor*," the boy told Agent Dioso, "they pay me to, wash two cars. One was a Buick and the other was a black Studebaker with white sidewall tires and license plates from Illinois. I remember well, because they made me wash the cars on the street in front of the hotel and they stayed there to watch me all the time."

Returning to the border the following day, April 13, the Customs men posted a description of the Studebaker automobile at all gates, with instructions to inspectors to be on the alert for this car.

That evening Lamar had a telephone call from an Immigration Service inspector also stationed at the border. "I saw your lookout notice for the Studebaker," the inspector said. "I think that car must have driven through before you posted the description, because it's parked in front of my apartment house on Grant Avenue."

Lamar and Dioso met the Immigration Service man at his apartment and went to the street to look at the Studebaker from a distance. "Tonight," Lamar said, "when the street is deserted, will you feel around under the car and let me know if you find anything unusual?"

It was after midnight when the Immigration inspector reported. "The whole bottom of the car is filled with cellophane packages," he said.

For two days Customs agents kept a night-and-day watch on the Studebaker to see who might drive it away. Nobody came. On April 15 the Customs men seized the car and found about sixty pounds of prepared marijuana concealed by metal plates similar to those found under the Buick. Inside the Studebaker several latent fingerprints were "lifted" by the identification expert of the Laredo Police Department. Most important was the discovery of several papers showing that the car was owned by Tomas Garcia of Chicago, jointly with Francisco and Lolita Garcia. There was also an affidavit made by Tomas Garcia to the effect that he had loaned the car to his brother Francisco for a trip to Mexico.

On April 16 the Customs men again talked with Lolita

in the county jail, showing her the papers which proved she was part owner of the Studebaker.

"Now do you want to tell us the story?" Lamar asked. "The real story?"

She nodded slowly. "I tell you."

She told them that Francisco had telephoned her in Chicago asking if she wanted to visit her children, who were living with his parents in Mexico City. She had traveled with him to Mexico City in the Studebaker, and stayed with his mother and father for almost four weeks, during which he and Juan Perfidio lived at the Hotel Canada.

When they left Mexico City the three drove to Nuevo Laredo and stayed at the Hotel Flores. Francisco and Juan, she said, talked with some stranger there, and when it came time to leave for the United States, Francisco and Lolita rode in the Studebaker, while Juan drove his own Buick. At the border, however, Francisco and Lolita stopped and watched Juan as he was questioned by the Customs inspectors. They saw him taken into the station for questioning, and they saw the inspectors chase him and search the Buick and find the marijuana. Francisco then drove back to Nuevo Laredo immediately, and there he put Lolita in the taxicab to return to the United States while he stayed in Mexico. Apparently he had decided later to drive the Studebaker back to Laredo and leave it.

"Where is Francisco now?" Lamar asked.

"I don't know. Maybe in Nuevo Laredo," she said.

"If he's there, will you try to persuade him to come here and meet you?"

She gazed through the barred windows for a few minutes. "Si," she said, "I will help you."

With the permission of their superior officers in Houston and the United States Attorney in Laredo, the Customs agents took Lolita in the custody of a police matron to a

hotel room in Laredo. There she telephoned the Hotel
Flores in Nuevo Laredo. Francisco was there.

"Where are you?" he asked.

She mentioned the name of the hotel.

"Is everything all right?"

"Yes. You come over and meet me here tonight. Okay?"

"All right. You stay there."

Throughout the night and the next morning the agents
and the matron kept their vigil in the hotel, but no further
word came from Francisco, and Lolita was returned to the
jail. An agent was stationed in the hotel just in case Francisco should turn up.

Francisco didn't turn up. In fact, he apparently vanished.
The agents established that he had disappeared from
Nuevo Laredo after he had talked with Lolita by telephone, and all efforts to pick up his trail were fruitless. It
appeared that he may have sneaked across the border at
some distant point.

"Sometime," Lamar said, "sometime—maybe not tomorrow or the next day—but sometime he'll go back to his old
hangouts in Chicago. And when he does, we'll be waiting
for him."

It was a long wait, but on September 13, exactly five
months after the arrest of Juan Perfidio, Francisco Garcia
was taken into custody by Customs agents in Chicago,
turned over to the United States Marshal and ordered removed to Texas for prosecution.

Francisco refused to identify the person or persons from
whom he bought the marijuana, or those to whom it was
to be sold in Chicago. However, when Juan Perfidio learned
that Francisco had been arrested, he sent for Lamar.

"I will tell you about the Chicago connection if you
will help me get off," Juan said.

"I can't do that," Lamar replied. "I can't promise you
anything, because only the court can decide what will

happen to you. But I'll tell you this—if you do make a statement to me, I'll see that the court knows you were of help to the government, and I'm sure that will be taken into consideration."

Juan implicated a notorious Chicago gangster Charlie Catrine, who was a suspected dealer in narcotics. Catrine had sent Francisco a telegraphic money order for three hundred dollars to buy the marijuana in Mexico.

The money order was located and Catrine was arrested by Customs and Narcotic agents in Chicago, but he denied any knowledge of the marijuana smuggling. Yes, he knew Francisco and Juan. Yes, he had loaned money to Juan occasionally for gambling purposes, and he had sent three hundred dollars to Francisco in Mexico, but purely as a personal loan.

Catrine, Francisco and Juan were brought to trial in Laredo, Texas, in March. Catrine and Francisco pleaded not guilty, while Juan kept his promise to help the government by telling the truth about the smuggling conspiracy. Lolita also testified for the government. The trial lasted three days, but the jury deliberated for only ten minutes. The verdict: Guilty as to Catrine, Francisco and Juan. The case against Lolita was dismissed upon recommendation of the government.

Charlie Catrine was sentenced to prison for ten years, Francisco for seven and Juan to two years and six months.

The evidence, two hundred and one pounds of prepared marijuana, was set aside to be destroyed, as is done in all such cases when they are definitely closed.

This is the kind of smuggling case which the Customs inspectors and Customs agents take in their stride day in and day out—no blood and thunder, no shooting, no Hollywood dramatics, but a job which is of vital importance to every American.

Just as important in another way is the unusual work

done by agents of another Treasury enforcement agency, the Alcohol and Tobacco Tax Division of the Internal Revenue Service, which has two big responsibilities: Fighting moonshiners and bootleggers, and enforcing the National Firearms Act and the Federal Firearms Act. How do they go about these jobs, and what do they accomplish?

11

MOONSHINE MONKEYSHINES

In the Tennessee mountains a group of state officers poked through heavy woods and brush to raid a still for the production of homemade whisky. (A "still" is another name for "distillery"—it is simply an apparatus for distilling alcohol.) When finally they arrived at the cedar grove where the still was in operation they discovered that the moonshiners had fled, and there was no one to greet the raiding party except a drunken mouse that had been tippling in the barrel of fermented mash used to make the whisky!

As the men approached, the little mouse sat up on the edge of the barrel and poked its head with one paw, as if it were saluting the officers.

The fire was still burning under the still, and eleven barrels of "mountain dew" were being "aged" under the trees. The officers destroyed the mash and the brew, but were unable to identify or arrest the people responsible for making it.

In another case in Kentucky, a deputy sheriff went squirrel hunting and suddenly heard the loud screams of a pig in distress. Approaching a small clearing he found a large sow struggling in a barrel of moonshine mash as five or six little piglets scampered around her. She had climbed into the barrel and couldn't get out, and when the deputy sheriff tipped the barrel over and released her, she staggered away in a daze—a hiccuping hog!

One North Carolina moonshiner kept his still in a corral with fifty dirty hound dogs. Mash, while cooking, has a strong odor which can sometimes lead officers to an illicit distillery, so this man had set up his equipment in the dog yard because the smell of the animals was so overpowering that it completely concealed the odor of the mash! To make it worse, he had thrown huge chunks of rotting horse meat into the pen as food for the hounds, and the mash he used for his liquor was crawling with flies and maggots. Officers eventually located the filthy still, destroyed the mash and whisky and arrested the owner.

Like most other makers of illicit liquor, this operator wasn't bothered by the fact that his product, made of filthy materials in filthy containers in a filthy location, might harm or even kill people who were foolish enough to buy and drink it. Most moonshiners have no regard for the welfare of customers, for society in general, or for the government. Vats of mash are often homes for rats and vermin. Homemade whisky is often poured into bottles which have been thrown into dumps, garbage cans, or other unsanitary places. Some operators are known to have mixed shellac-thinner, wood alcohol or other poisons with their liquor to make it "go further."

Not all illicit distilleries make poison or harmful liquor, however, and not all are one-man or amateur installations. Some operators, in fact, make whisky which tastes as good as some sold in legitimate trade, and some illicit distilleries are elaborate and well equipped, requiring several men to supervise production.

Production of whisky and alcohol in some one hundred and eighty-four *legal* distilleries may total as much as five hundred million gallons a year, and the annual revenue collected by the government from these companies may be two *billion* dollars or more.

No one really knows how much illicit liquor is made every year, but more than nine hundred agents of the Alcohol and Tobacco Tax Division (ATTD) of the Internal Revenue Service seize a yearly average of ten thousand stills and arrest as many moonshiners. State and local police reportedly seize another estimated six thousand or more annually.

Even if each of the ten thousand illicit distilleries produced only one hundred gallons each (and some produce a great deal more than that), the estimated tax loss to the United States would be around ten and a half million dollars a year.

The seizures of illicit distilleries and arrests of their operators have two important results: They save an untold number of lives of people who might otherwise die or become seriously ill from drinking mixtures which are not fit for human use; and they keep the government from being defrauded of millions of dollars in taxes. This is the main responsibility of the ATTD—to enforce the Internal Revenue laws relating to liquor and alcohol.

The ATTD agents are known among some of the southern mountain folk as "revenooers," and in many isolated mountain areas it is considered quite proper to ambush and shoot at any stranger on the theory that he may be a "revenooer" searching for an illicit still. But the ATTD agent has his job to do, and like other Treasury agents, he does it sometimes at the risk of his life.

The problem of controlling the production of distilled spirits for purposes of revenue is not new. Wine and brandy were made in Europe in the Middle Ages, and whisky was manufactured in the peat huts of Ireland and in the Scotch highlands long before the Pilgrims landed in America.

The Pilgrims brought alcoholic beverages to the colonies, and the first American saloon opened in Boston in 1625. By 1633 the Massachusetts Bay Colony required saloon-keepers to buy liquor permits, and Connecticut followed in 1643. From that time forward, the production of distilled spirits in the United States has been subject to controls and the payment of taxes.

The first Internal Revenue law, enacted March 3, 1791, imposed a distillery tax of fifty-four cents per gallon of the still capacity, and an additional seven cents for each gallon of whisky produced. In 1959 the Internal Revenue tax was ten dollars and fifty cents for each proof gallon produced.

There was tremendous opposition to the first federal whisky tax, especially in Pennsylvania, where hundreds of farmers raised so much grain that it could not be sold in the market. Therefore, they used the unsold crops to make and sell a kind of whisky called Monongahela, named for the principal river in that area. It was not fair, they said, for the government to tax this whisky on which they depended for their very existence, and some seven thousand of these farmers decided to band together to fight the tax collection. Modern history books refer to this fight as the Whisky Rebellion or the Whisky Insurrection.

The rebellion was no mild affair. When the tax collector for the counties of Allegheny and Washington started out to make his collections, he was waylaid near Pigeon Creek by a group of armed and masked men who shaved off his hair, covered him with hot tar and feathers and took his horse.

When the collector finally limped into town and reported

to the authorities, a deputy marshal was assigned to track down the attackers. When the deputy failed to return, a search party went looking for him. He was found blindfolded and tied to a tree in a dense forest. He had been horsewhipped, tarred and feathered, then left to die.

A few of the rebellious farmers were arrested, but others kidnaped and beat the persons who could testify against them in court, so that convictions were impossible.

President George Washington issued a proclamation condemning the lawless acts of the whisky-makers, and warning them to stop their opposition, but the proclamation only served to make the rebels more bitter. In a different approach, Washington then issued two new orders, one directing that all distilled spirits in the rebellious counties were to be seized on their way to market, and the other requiring that the Army buy only spirits on which the duty had been paid.

The insurrectionists stepped up their campaign under the direction of the chief agitator David Bradford, a wealthy and unscrupulous landowner of Washington County. They burned the barns of distillers who paid the taxes, and destroyed their distilleries. They broke into homes, wrecked farm machinery, threatened the lives of law-abiding people, and even robbed the mails to read letters to learn the identities of those who sympathized with the government.

In August Bradford assembled seven thousand armed men, proposing to lead them on a march to Pittsburgh to attack Fort Pitt, seize the United States arsenal and establish an independent nation. This bold plan apparently frightened them, for the attack never took place. Bradford, however, continued to recruit new allies until he had an army of sixteen thousand men who pledged themselves to help him resist the government and fight the whisky tax.

President Washington's patience was finally exhausted.

He was faced with two choices. He could let the rebellion grow, or he could use force to end it. On August 7 he issued a proclamation which, in effect, ordered all the rebels to disperse and retire to their homes by September 1, or face whatever force was needed to restore law and order to the land.

David Bradford ridiculed the President's ultimatum. "I could marshal an army that would scatter Washington's forces to the four winds. Let 'em come! We'll show them what our motto means—*Liberty and No Excise, No Asylum for Cowards and Traitors!*"

Washington took up the challenge by mobilizing fifteen thousand militiamen from New Jersey, Pennsylvania, Maryland and Virginia, under the command of General Henry Lee, Governor of Virginia. When this determined army marched across the Alleghenies and descended upon the rebel strongholds, the insurgents quickly surrendered. Bradford and other leaders fled the state, and although several hundred prisoners were captured they were later pardoned by the President after they agreed to obey the law and keep the peace.

The Whisky Rebellion was important, not because of the opposition to the payment of taxes, but because it marked the first time that the full power of the federal government was brought to bear to enforce the federal laws within the states. The contest, in Washington's own words, decided "whether a small proportion of the United States shall dictate to the whole Union."

Today the fight against illicit distilleries continues, and some of the stills seized by the ATTD in Pennsylvania may even be operated by descendants of the "Whisky Rebels." Most of the illicit distilling in Pennsylvania is in the eastern part of the state, and it is rather extensive. Mr. Thomas Bailey, Chief of the Enforcement Branch of the ATTD, points out that about ninety-eight per cent of outlaw whisky is produced in only one fifth of the geographical area of the United States—in Kentucky, Virginia, Tennessee, North and South Carolina, Mississippi, Alabama, Georgia, Florida, eastern Pennsylvania, all of New Jersey and the metropolitan areas of New York, including Brooklyn and Long Island. The worst state in the country for moonshine violations is North Carolina, where ATTD agents seize as many as four hundred illicit stills a month!

The ATTD gets valuable help from the Coast Guard, another Treasury agency, which uses its aircraft to detect illicit stills from the air, especially in several southern states. In one such case in Alabama the Coast Guard pilot talked by radio with ATTD agents on the ground.

"Your target is due east about one mile," he reported. "I can see two men in the woods and there's a third man on the ridge about a hundred yards away. Seems to be a lookout."

Agents Scott Jones and Frank Candler left their car on the highway and trudged eastward into the woods. "We'll have to get the lookout first," Jones said. "Keep your eyes open for him."

As they approached the ridge which concealed the still, Candler held out one arm to stop Jones. Candler pointed to his left. There on the hill they could see a man in overalls sitting on a log.

"Has he got a gun?" Jones asked.

"I don't see any, but he must have some way of warning the others."

Under cover of the trees the agents crept forward toward the sentinel. They went within fifty feet of where he sat without being detected. There they lay in the brush and made whispered plans.

"Look, Scott," Candler said, "can you see those two wires hanging over the branch behind that guy?"

Jones saw the wires and both men guessed their purpose.

The wires were connected to some sort of warning device near the still. All the lookout had to do was touch them together, or push a button, and the warning would sound. The agents could not get to the still without going past the man on watch, so they crept toward him slowly, depending on the bushes and trees for concealment. When they were only about thirty feet away Jones gave the signal and they jumped up and ran toward the man.

Hearing the noise, he leaped to his feet and faced the agents. By the time he started to move for the wires, the two were upon him, covering his mouth so he couldn't call out.

Leaving Candler with the gagged lookout, Jones followed the electric wires, which were strung loosely through the trees, to a spot about two hundred feet from the place where the lookout had been posted. At the ends of the wires he saw a jar suspended about five feet from the ground—a jar containing five sticks of dynamite! Had the watchman connected the wires there would have been a terrific explosion and the moonshiners would have fled.

Jones disconnected the wires and kept pushing forward until he could see the still and the two men who were operating it. One was about twenty-five years old, the other in his forties. Jones crept to the clearing and suddenly stood up and showed himself.

"Hold everything!" he shouted. "You're under arrest."

The younger man was too surprised to move. His companion, however, began to run, and Jones went into action at the same moment. He grabbed the young man, handcuffed him to a tree, then dashed after the one in flight.

Now it was Jones's turn to be surprised, for he saw his quarry dive into a hole in the ground and disappear. When Jones reached the hole he found it to be about four feet in diameter and about fifteen feet deep, and at the bottom

he could see and hear an underground stream. There was
no sign of the man.

Quickly he noted that the stream flowed to his right. He
ran in that direction, jumping through bushes and over
fallen logs, until he came to a sheer cliff some twenty feet
high. At the bottom he could see a sizable mountain stream,
the same stream that flowed through the hole where the
moonshiner disappeared.

The agent could not risk making the twenty-foot jump,
and there did not seem to be any other way to descend
safely, yet he had to get down there because he was
sure the fugitive would soon emerge in the water. At the
edge of the bluff Jones noticed a tall sapling. He made a
running jump and grabbed the trunk of the tree as high up
as he could. The tree bent over and the agent lowered himself through its branches until he was about eight feet
above the stream. He let go and landed only a foot or two
from the water. His move was made none too soon, because from the opening in the cliff came the fleeing moonshiner, who stood up wiping the water from his face and
sucking in deep breaths of air. Blinking incredulously, he
stared at Jones.

"Where'd you come from, boy?" he asked. "I figured I
left you at the still." He shook his head and added, "I
swear—you revenooers ain't human, you ain't."

Another moonshine case succeeded because of an agent's
passion for perfection. In Tennessee, ATTD Agent George
Bastian, together with Jim Cox of the state's Beverage
Control Department, raided a house in which they had
reason to believe a still was in operation. Bastian had been
in the ATTD for only a little more than a year. Cox was an
old-timer.

On the way to the house in Cox's car, Bastian wiped the
dust from the dashboard with one hand. "Dashboards are
always dusty," he said. Cox merely laughed.

A few minutes later Bastian leaned forward and picked a rubber band off the floor mat. "You might need this sometime," he said, and opened the dash compartment to put the rubber band away. He straightened up some maps and papers in the compartment and Cox laughed again.

"Are you nervous, kid, or just particular?"

Bastian smiled. "I'm not nervous. I'm always doing things like that. My wife says I'm a perfectionist—you know, a place for everything and everything in its place."

When they reached the house and served their search warrant they inspected the place from top to bottom without finding any evidence of illegal whisky. As they prepared to leave, Bastian noticed a calendar on the wall near the entrance. It was an ordinary advertising calendar with a colorful picture of a scantily dressed girl, but it was hanging crooked. Cox was standing near the door.

"Just a second," Bastian said. "I'll be right with you." He moved the calendar so that it hung straight—and as he did so, he detected the faint smell of whisky. Sliding the calender aside, he discovered a hole in the wall and a small faucet attached to a copper tube. He turned the faucet, a thin stream of liquid touched his fingers. It was moonshine.

"What about this?" he said to the owner.

The owner stared at the faucet and merely shrugged his shoulders. Bastian and Cox found that the copper tube led to a hidden storage space under the roof where the tube was connected to a keg of illicit whisky. Beside the keg were eight five-gallon jugs, all empty.

As they took their evidence and prisoner out of the house, Bastian straightened the calendar again and Cox snickered. "A place for everything, huh?" Cox said.

ATTD agents often have to think fast and act quickly. In one case in Georgia two agents had under surveillance a large truck being loaded with sugar which they suspected was to be driven to a big illicit distillery. The location of the distillery was unknown, and if the agents should follow the truck too closely they would probably be discovered, especially if the truck traveled through isolated territory.

Soon the truck was loaded and it pulled away from the loading platform. The agents followed at a discreet distance. When finally they were out on the open road, the agents' car went close to the truck, and when it slowed down in climbing a steep hill, one agent managed to leave his car and run to the truck on foot. With a jackknife he reached up and cut a small hole in one of the sugar sacks.

As suspected, the truck did turn off the main highway and drive through flat, open country—but the driver did not see any cars following him, because the ATTD men were far behind, following a thin trail of sugar which spilled from the cut sack. The trail led to the illicit distillery, which the agents seized. It had a capacity of four hundred gallons a day and had already produced more than ten thousand gallons of bootleg whisky, representing a tax fraud of more than one hundred thousand dollars.

Some cases developed by the ATTD have their humorous side. Treasury agents, being human, sometimes make mistakes, occasionally with unusual results. Once two young ATTD agents, summoned unexpectedly to participate in a mass raid, reported late and were not adequately briefed about operational plans. They drove to the designated town, spied a warehouse with a sign bearing the offender's name they had been given, and descended upon the building.

Since the owner was present, they displayed their credentials and asked his permission to make a search. He consented. Digging into a miniature mountain of grain, the two agents discovered that it concealed one thousand five hundred gallons of alcohol. They took the owner and the evidence back to their headquarters, where they proudly reported to their supervisor.

"That's fine," he told them. "You made only one mistake."

"What was that?" they asked.

"You raided the wrong place!"

They had stumbled upon a warehouse belonging to a man of the same name as the one they were supposed to arrest. As it turned out, the right man was also taken into custody, and both he and the bootlegger arrested by mistake were convicted and sentenced.

In another case, ATTD agents concealed their car in heavy brush at right angles to a highway to await the passage of an automobile believed to be transporting a load of illicit liquor. According to their information the car, with two or three men, would drive past their location about two o'clock in the morning.

At that hour they saw the headlights of an automobile driving at high speed in their direction. They flashed on the lights of their car and prepared for action, expecting that the oncoming driver would try to stop and turn around, or get out and run. Instead, however, the speeding vehicle slowed down and stopped beside the agents. The driver promptly asked whether or not he could be of any assistance. On the seat beside him the agents saw a fashionably dressed girl.

Believing they had stopped the wrong car, the agents waved the driver on and settled back to wait for the liquor carrier—which never came. It was not until much later that they learned the car they had stopped was indeed "loaded," and that the beautiful girl in the front seat had been a department store dummy! They finally arrested their man under other circumstances.

Another girl, a real one this time, was the cause of red faces on six ATTD agents who swept down a hillside to capture a gang of moonshiners. The agents were concealed on a wooded rise, where they used binoculars to watch the operators of the still. In addition to five male moonshiners, the agents saw a beautiful young girl, scantily clad in shorts—Daisy Mae of Dogpatch come to life. When it came time for the raid, all of the agents rushed to take the girl into custody—and the five men got away! They were later rounded up and brought to trial.

Like other Treasury enforcement agents, the ATTD investigators face danger and death in the performance of their duties. Between May 10, 1934, and April 1, 1958, eleven ATTD men were killed by gunfire, four hundred and sixty-six were beaten or assaulted by violators—and forty-five violators were killed by the investigators.

A closed case from the ATTD files shows how a casual inquiry may turn into a tragedy. As in other cases in this book, the names used are fictitious but the facts are not colored in any way.

On a March morning William Smart and Frank Farley, two ATTD investigators, met two investigators employed by the Alabama Alcoholic Beverage Control (ABC) Board, Robert Bruce and Ralph Smith. The ATTD men had confidential information that a large unregistered distillery was in operation near "the Johnson place" on a huge planta-tion owned by Will Love in Monroe County, Alabama, and they had asked the ABC agents to help them locate the still.

The four drove to the sprawling plantation and came to a fork in the road, where they stopped the car.

"I think we should take the right-hand road," Ralph Smith said. "We've broken up some stills down there in the past."

They took the right-hand road, passing an occupied house where a colored man was seated on a bench on the front porch. Tracks in the dirt indicated that no cars had turned off the road into the yard, so they did not stop at this house. According to their information there was a great deal of vehicular travel wherever the distillery was located.

They continued down the dirt road, looking for tire tracks or other clues, but they finally came to an open field where the road ended, and they decided to backtrack. Returning to the house where they had seen the Negro on the porch, they saw that he was no longer there, but the door was open and they could hear music from a radio inside the place.

"Somebody's in there," Smart said.

Agent Farley blew the car horn, but no one appeared.

"There's a cooker," Smart said, pointing to a can under which a small fire burned in the yard. It was a "still-cooker," used by small manufacturers of moonshine. "Blow the horn again, Frank."

Farley sounded the horn and the Negro they had previously seen came out and sat on a bench near the open door. "Can you tell us where the Johnson place is?" Farley called.

The man shook his head. "You're on the wrong road."

"Well, can you tell us where it is?"

"Go back to the highway and turn right."

"How far is it?"

"I don't know. I ain't measured it." The Negro then asked, "Is Mr. Love with you-all?"

"No, he isn't," Farley answered.

The colored man leaned forward and squinted, trying to see who was in the car. Suddenly, without straightening up, he wheeled and rushed into the house, slamming the door.

"He's going out the back door!" Farley exclaimed. "He's probably going to pour out something!"

Farley jumped from the car and ran to the back of the house, but no one was in sight. From inside the shack he heard a woman's voice pleading, "Don't do that, George —don't!" Then he heard the sound of a gunshot.

Farley sped up the steps to the kitchen door and opened

it. Instantly a big mongrel hound grabbed the agent's trouser leg in his teeth, pulling and growling. Farley kicked the animal, who screeched and let go, slinking into a corner of the room.

There was no one else in the kitchen, so the agent hurried to a door leading into the front of the house. Just as he reached for the doorknob he heard another blast of gunfire, and as he burst into the room he saw the Negro standing at the front entrance, lowering a shotgun from his shoulder. Close by the door stood an elderly colored woman, later identified as the man's mother. She was crying.

George Drake, the Negro, turned to face Farley, who grabbed him and began to wrestle for the shotgun. In the scuffle Farley heard a pistol shot outside the shack, and actually heard the bullet sing past his ear.

"Don't shoot in here!" he yelled. "I've got him! Don't shoot!"

Drake continued to struggle and to hold the shotgun. At one point he tried to get a shell from his pocket, apparently intending to load the weapon and kill the agent, but Farley prevented it. In a few moments Bruce rushed in and he and Farley wrested the gun away from Drake and handcuffed the prisoner.

"He shot Bill Smart," Bruce said.

Farley looked startled, then ran to the front porch, where he found Smart bleeding profusely from a shotgun wound in the groin. Farley tried to stanch the flow with a handkerchief, but it was too late. Smart died in less than two minutes.

Farley walked slowly back into the house and stared at George Drake. "Why did you do that?" he said, pointing at Smart's body.

Drake kept shaking his head as he looked down at the floor. "I don't know why I shot that man," he said.

The agents seized Drake's illicit still, part of which he

kept in his pigpen. He admitted that he had been making beer and whisky for about four months. Within six months after the murder of Agent Smart, George Drake was convicted of murder in the second degree in federal court at Mobile, Alabama, and was sentenced to serve ten years in a federal penitentiary.

Not all of the dramatic cases in the ATTD files are centered around the activities of operators of illicit distilleries. The ATTD has another important function which is of vital importance to every law-abiding American—the enforcement of the National Firearms Act and the Federal Firearms Act, which help to keep dangerous weapons out of the hands of criminals and delinquents. The men who do this job, involving the seizure of sawed-off shotguns, Tommy guns and other murderous firearms, strike at the very heart of underworld violence. They work hand in hand with state and local police departments, and we have selected a dramatic adventure to show how this close co-operation effectively removes modern gunslingers and potential killers from our cities and towns.

12

TRICKS AND TRIGGERS

In the Prohibition Era, when wines, beer and liquor were outlawed, underworld gang empires prospered in the bootlegging business, but each gang lord had to fight tough competition. Violence was a partner in the black market, and murders were committed with growing frequency and bold defiance of the law. Thugs with submachine guns massacred their opposition in broad daylight on city streets. Sawed-off shotguns were hidden under suit coats until the wearers were given the signal to yank them out and blast away. Virtually every gangster carried an automatic pistol or a revolver and was ready to use it freely to eliminate a competitor, a witness, a nosy policeman, a federal agent or any other enemy of gangland.

When Prohibition ended, the crime syndicates turned to kidnaping, bank robbery and other offenses, still depending heavily upon their arsenals to back up threats of violence and to "rub out" those brave enough to stand in their way.

In 1934 Congress passed the National Firearms Act,

designed to keep fully automatic firearms and sawed-off shotguns from getting into the hands of criminals. The act requires the registration (with the Commissioner of Internal Revenue) of all machine guns, machine pistols, and sawed-off shotguns or rifles having a barrel less than eighteen inches long, with the exception of .22 (or smaller) caliber rifles if the barrel is sixteen inches or more in length. Each weapon must be registered by its owner; and if it is transferred to another person, the one who makes the transfer is required to pay a special transfer tax of two hundred dollars to the government, or he may go to prison for five years.

In 1938, realizing the need for additional firearms legislation to cope with crime, Congress passed the Federal Firearms Act, which prohibits a person from shipping or receiving firearms or ammunition in interstate or foreign commerce if that person has been convicted of a crime of violence, or is under indictment for such a crime, or is a fugitive from justice. This law also makes it illegal for any person or concern to ship firearms or ammunition in interstate or foreign commerce to the type of individual mentioned above; or to ship, receive, store or sell in interstate or foreign commerce any stolen firearm or ammunition; or to ship or receive in interstate or foreign commerce any firearm from which the manufacturer's serial number has been removed, obliterated or altered.

The enforcement of these laws was delegated to the Alcohol and Tobacco Tax Division because of the revenue provisions in the laws, and the job suddenly became a terrific burden when, during World War II, men in our armed forces brought or sent back to this country thousands of assorted fully automatic weapons, such as submachine guns and machine pistols. Some of the guns were put away in attics or closets, only to be discovered there by curious small children in the family, who pulled triggers and died.

A special Revenue agent whose real name is Henry Schneider, now Deputy Director of Information for the Internal Revenue Service, planned and directed a campaign to educate owners of such guns to turn them in to be deactivated—that is, to be made harmless. By 1948 more than a million weapons were turned in, deactivated and returned to their owners as harmless souvenirs. Statisticians estimate that this program has saved about a thousand lives each year, and Henry Schneider earned the personal thanks of President Harry S. Truman "for saving thousands of lives and millions of dollars."

Unfortunately, a weapon which has been deactivated can be put back in working order by replacing damaged parts, and some criminals sought to evade the firearms law by buying the harmless guns and having them rebuilt by unscrupulous gunsmiths.

Actually, most of the cases involving violations of the firearms laws are adopted by the ATTD from local police departments, sheriffs and state police units, because most of the violations first come to light when some local or state law has been broken. Sometimes it is difficult or impossible for the states to convict criminals on state charges where violent crimes have been committed with firearms —but this does not mean that they go free, for the federal government prosecutes them under the federal firearms laws.

One outstanding case which shows how this co-operation succeeds took place in Tennessee, where an interstate syndicate of hijackers used an arsenal of submachine guns, .30 caliber carbines, revolvers and automatic pistols in a dramatic robbery spree. In this story, only the names are fictitious.

One of the first raids made by the robbers took place three days before Christmas, 1949, about midnight, in the back room of a club run by Orville Duke near Henderson,

Kentucky. Let Orville tell part of the story in his own words:

I was engaged in a dice game in the rear of my place of business. I saw my bartender being shoved back into the room where I was by a man afterward identified as Tony Balotto. He had an air-cooled-type submachine gun. He said, "Stick 'em up!" and pointed the gun at us. Then I saw another man enter the room from the outside door. He had a blue steel pistol in his hand. I have identified this man as Joe Neece. He forced a cab driver named Tom inside, then hit him with a pistol, knocking him down. He kicked him in the ribs and tried to kick him in the face while he was on the floor.

(Other men came in to cover the crowd with guns.) About that time a guard, stationed in a concealed place up next to the ceiling behind the partition, fired one shot from a twenty-gauge shotgun. His charge struck the wall next to an unidentified man carrying a machine gun. All became very nervous and a second shot was fired by the guard. This charge struck the unidentified holdup man in the right side, causing him to bend over.

He said, "Boys, they got me!"

He attempted to raise his gun and fire. He only discharged one shot before his gun hung on him.

Tony Balotto stepped back behind the partition and emptied his submachine gun. I later counted about thirty-two holes in the wall.

Balotto called outside and Vince Clapham came in. He told Clapham, "Pick up that money. I've

already taken care of that ——— ——— ——— up
there."

Joe Neece helped the wounded man out of the
door to the parking lot. Balotto left the room by
the front door and fired a shot into the ceiling.
Those of us present remained in the room for two
or three minutes.

The dice players estimated that the cash which the
bandits took from the playing table totaled about eight
thousand five hundred dollars. But some of the dice players
were destined to see the robbers again and to lose more
money.

On May 21, 1950, about five o'clock in the afternoon,
a chicken fight was in progress at a barn on the Ohio River
in Henderson County, Kentucky, when six men walked in,
five of them wearing dark raincoats and masks made from
handkerchiefs. The sixth man, who was unmasked, was
Tony Balotto. Two of his companions were later identified
as Joe Neece and Vince Clapham. Tony and Joe were
armed with submachine guns. Clapham carried a pistol.

"Get 'em up!" Balotto ordered. The gamblers raised
their hands and Balotto then instructed them to line up.

"Where's Orville Duke?" Balotto asked. "I was told he
was here." No one answered, and Balotto lifted the submachine gun. "I said where's Duke?"

One of the men answered, "He's not here. He left over
an hour ago." The gambler who spoke was Orville Duke.

"That's tough," Balotto said. "But I'll find him someplace.
He's the mug that's the cause of one of my buddies gettin'
killed." He came close to the line of victims. "Now you
guys listen," he said. "We was out at Duke's place not long
ago and somebody said later that we overlooked more
money than we got. The boys had it stashed in their pockets.

So all you big gamblers just unbutton your pants and pull
'em off. Come on, now—move!"

The men removed their trousers, which one of the robbers put over his arm.

Curly Grant, one of the men in the line, wore a diamond
ring which the bandits seized, but they overlooked three
thousand four hundred dollars which he had stuffed in his
socks.

"Whose Cadillac is that parked near the door?" one
of the holdup men asked.

The men looked at each other and one said, "That's
Curly Grant's."

"Step out, Curly Grant," the bandit ordered. Curly didn't
move.

"Come on, come on! Step out before I get rough!"

One of the victims spoke up. "Go ahead, Curly, give him
the car keys so they can leave."

Curly produced the keys and the men drove away in his
Cadillac. When the car was later recovered, Curly found
that another two thousand five hundred dollars which he
had wrapped in a newspaper was still in the trunk of the
car. The only thing missing was a .38 caliber Smith &
Wesson revolver which he had left on the seat.

Balotto and his accomplices laid low for a time, but on
September 12, about four months after the chicken-fight
holdup, they made another "score." The scene was the
Ranger Club in Henderson County, Kentucky. Mrs. Betty
Harper, cashier and bookkeeper for the club, was working
in her office on the second floor when she heard a knock on
the door and opened it. Tony Balotto strode in, followed
by a tall, slim man wearing a mask. Both held shiny pistols.

"This is a holdup, lady," Balotto said.

Mrs. Harper laughed. "Don't be silly."

"Don't you be silly," the tall man said.

They walked into two adjoining rooms to see if anyone

was there. Mrs. Harper returned to her desk and resumed work on her accounts. "If you're satisfied you can get out," she told them.

Behind Mrs. Harper's desk was the office safe, its door standing open. Balotto started toward it. Mrs Harper reached out to close the safe door and Balotto swung his left fist, striking the woman in the jaw. The tall man grabbed her left arm and twisted it behind her, forcing her into an adjoining room. She kicked and struggled so much that Balotto stepped in. "Take that troublemaker downstairs," he commanded.

Still holding her arm, the masked man pushed Mrs. Harper toward the stairs. At the top step she tried to trip him but failed, and when they reached the bottom he slapped her across the face and made her line up with the other club employees.

Standing near the bar was Vince Clapham, who waved his gun at the employees and said, "You're all lucky we ain't amatchoors in this racket. If we was, some of you would prob'ly be hurtin' bad by this time."

Elsie Hankins, one of the women who worked for the club, suddenly broke away and ran out the door. In the yard she saw an automobile with a man sitting in the front seat. She rushed to the car, got in quickly and turned terrified eyes to the driver.

"Quick, mister!" she cried. "Get away from here! They're holdin' up the place. They got guns!"

One of the bandits who had chased Elsie saw that she was in the car and he called to the driver, "Take care of her, Eddie."

"Okay," Eddie answered. "She'll be okay."

Elsie stared at him in fright. "You—you're one of 'em!" she cried.

Eddie Hines smiled. "You're scared to death, aren't you?"

"Yes, *sir!*"

"This the first time you've been in anything like this?"

"It sure is—and I hope it's the last time, too."

"Well, you just sit still and don't look at me—and you'll be all right," he said, patting her on the shoulder. A few minutes later Vince Clapham came out and took Elsie back into the club.

After cleaning out the safe and taking the cash and jewelry from their victims, the gang departed. The state police were notified, but a search failed to reveal the whereabouts of Balotto and his companions. They had vanished.

On the night of November 26 a dark green 1949 Oldsmobile sedan was stolen in Chicago, Illinois, and was reported to Chicago police. This theft was to be linked to Tony Balotto and his boys in a dramatic fashion.

On November 27 a lieutenant and a patrolman from the Tennessee Highway Patrol saw a dark green 1949 Oldsmobile sedan parked near the Crown Club in Tipton County, Tennessee. The officers noticed the same car in the same place for several days, and one afternoon they stopped at the Crown Club and asked the bartender who owned the Oldsmobile.

"Oh," he said, "that belongs to a friend of mine. He's looking around for a job, and I told him it was okay for him to leave his car here. He'll be picking it up in a few days."

The officers looked at the license plate, noting that it was issued in Tennessee.

The reappearance of Tony Balotto's gang was as violent as its other performances had been. On December 4, about 6:45 P.M., a man named Roger C. Stanton, of Holly Springs, Mississippi, drove to the Grayhound Club near Byhalia, Mississippi, not far from the Tennessee border. Mr. Stanton was merely seeking some relaxation, but he found something quite the opposite.

Before he turned off his motor a man with a blue polka

dot handkerchief covering his face stepped up, shoved the barrel of a machine gun against Mr. Stanton's head and said, "Okay, Buster, get out."

Stanton got out and was "escorted" to the club entrance, where another man took him in tow. Inside the club he saw two more gangsters, one with a revolver, the other with a machine gun. The one with the revolver grabbed him by the collar.

"Where's your money?"

"I—I don't have any money."

The gangster raised his gun and whipped it across Stanton's mouth. His lips began to bleed and he spat out a tooth. He produced his wallet, which the gunman grabbed, finding that it contained about four hundred dollars.

Then the gangster patted Stanton on the shoulder. "Your mouth is bleeding," he said. "Come on, I'll take you to the washroom and we'll fix it up."

The robbery of the Grayhound Club was more thorough than the others. After seizing the cash in the club safe, the bandits remained in the club for about five hours. Joe Neece went outside and guided arriving patrons to parking places. Upon approaching the entrance, several of the customers noticed a green 1949 Oldsmobile sedan parked directly in front of the door.

Vince Clapham and another member of the gang named Dick Nutter acted as "inside doormen," and it was their job to relieve victims of their wallets and jewelry as they entered the clubroom. Tony Balotto and an accomplice named Jimmy Day guided the victims to chairs near the walls and made them sit quietly.

In the course of the evening, Tony made the club employees serve drinks and food to the robbery victims and also to him and his "boys."

In a search of the club Tony gathered up a rifle and

several revolvers, and with these and their loot (about twenty thousand dollars) the holdup men left about nine o'clock.

The club manager promptly called the Tennessee and Mississippi Highway Patrols to report the robbery. Captain Walter Lawford, together with Lieutenant William Stowe and Patrolman Rinkeley of the Tennessee Highway Patrol, sped to the club and talked with the victims. Several reported that the bandits escaped in a dark green 1949 Oldsmobile sedan bearing a Tennessee license beginning with the number "2."

Lieutenant Stowe said, "That sounds like the car I asked about at the Crown Club a few days ago. It's been parked there for a week."

"Let's go!" Captain Lawford said. They headed for the Crown Club, and on the way Captain Lawford radioed for another patrolman, Corporal Butler, to meet him there.

Meantime, a member of the Mississippi Highway Patrol, speeding by motorcycle to the scene of the robbery, passed a green Oldsmobile sedan near Holly Springs, Mississippi, headed toward Tennessee and traveling at "very high speed." The officer slammed on his brakes, turned as quickly as he could and set out after the speeding car. He failed to catch it.

At the Crown Club there was no sign of the 1949 Oldsmobile. Captain Lawford entered the club and talked with one of the proprietors, who claimed to be unable to furnish any information about the car or its owners.

As they started to leave, Captain Lawford happened to glance into a small room used as an office, where he saw four pieces of luggage, apparently brand new. He left the club with Lieutenant Stowe and gave orders to Corporal Butler and Patrolman Rinkeley. "Don't let anybody leave this place, and detain anyone who arrives here."

Butler and Rinkeley stationed themselves near the building behind the club's floodlights and waited. Butler was armed with a shotgun, Rinkeley with a Reising submachine gun. The first car drove in about 11:30 P.M. It was a green 1949 Oldsmobile sedan. The officers were instantly alert. The car stopped in the full glare of the floodlights and Butler could see three men in the front seat. Warily, Butler approached the car with his gun ready for action.

A cry came from Eddie Hines, the driver. "Don't shoot! Don't shoot! You got us. Don't shoot—please! Where's Johnny Knott? We can get this thing straightened out, Officer."

"Get out!" Butler commanded. "Keep your hands up."

The three men in the front seat climbed out. Butler yanked open the rear door and three men who had been covered by a tarpaulin came out sheepishly. On the floor of the car the corporal saw several guns and several white cloth bags which, upon examination, he found contained "a lot of money."

The officers sent a radio call to Captain Lawford, then lined up and searched the prisoners, finding that each carried a concealed revolver. Rinkeley kept his submachine gun pointed at them all the time and Joe Neece finally said, "Hey, will you get that machine gun off me? Now I know how those poor jerks felt while I had that oilcan pointed at them!"

Captain Lawford summoned the sheriff of Tipton County, Tennessee, and together they counted the money in the sacks. There was $11,368.19 in paper money and coins, as well as several men's and women's rings.

Among the firearms seized were a .45 caliber submachine gun of the "grease-gun" type, a Beretta submachine gun, two army carbines, a German Luger pistol, a .45 caliber automatic pistol, a .351 caliber Winchester rifle and several revolvers.

Eddie Hines asked to talk with the leader of the officers. When Captain Lawford said he was in charge, Hines said, "Can't we square this thing up?"

Lawford scowled. "You know better than that, punk. But don't worry—you'll have a long time to think, and this will give you something to think about."

"Yeh? Listen, copper," Eddie said, "you wouldn't have caught us napping exceptin' we was double-crossed. Johnny Knott was supposed to meet us in a jeep at the border and he didn't show. I'll tell you one thing, though—he ain't going to live this one down."

Because of the arsenal of weapons used by Balotto and his gang, the Tennessee authorities decided to turn the case over to the Alcohol and Tobacco Tax Division for federal prosecution under the National Firearms Act. Separate charges were also made for the theft of the Oldsmobile sedan, involving other violations of federal laws.

ATTD agents located and questioned Johnny Knott in Shelby County, Tennessee. Johnny, a one-time dice dealer in Illinois, said he had fifty thousand dollars invested as a partner in the Crown Club. What did he know about the robbery of the Grayhound Club?

"Don't know a thing about it," he told the agents.

"Just where were you on the fourth of December?" they asked.

"Well, now," he said, "you see I had a doggoned good bird dog and some sailor come along and stole him. I was over at Munford, and a fellow there told me he'd seen my dog near Collierville, so I went to Collierville to find him. That's where I was on the fourth of December—at Collierville, lookin' for my dog, and I can prove it."

"Were you driving a jeep?"

"Reckon I was."

The ATTD agents placed Johnny under arrest and he was brought to trial with the other six defendants in federal court in Memphis, Tennessee. In a way, Johnny Knott was lucky, for he got off with a sentence of only five years. The others—Tony Balotto, Eddie Hines, Jimmy Day, Joe Neece, Vince Clapham and Dick Nutter—were sentenced to serve fifteen years each.

The enforcement of the National Firearms Act and the Federal Firearms Act has not only been effective against gunmen and gangsters in the United States, but also has served to prevent the smuggling of guns and ammunition out of this country to rebel forces planning insurrections in neighboring republics. In such cases the ATTD works closely with the Customs Bureau and the United States Coast Guard, which is also a Treasury agency in peacetime. (In time of war it becomes a part of the United States Navy.)

The Coast Guard, as mentioned in our opening chapter, is America's oldest seagoing military service. In fighting gunrunners, smugglers and other lawbreakers, the Coast Guard is one of the strongest muscles in the powerful arm of Treasury law enforcement, working hand in hand, ashore and afloat, with all of the other Treasury crime fighters.

Asked to tell about one of its most exciting enforcement (nonmilitary)adventures for this book, the Coast Guard chose the story of a bloody battle on the high seas between the crew of a Coast Guard vessel and the crew of a "rum boat" during Prohibition—a battle in which two Coast Guardsmen were murdered along with a Secret Service agent who sacrificed his life to save the lives of his companions.

13

MURDER ON
THE HIGH SEAS

Because of the heroic actions involved in this case, the names of all the people are true.

On August 7, 1927, Secret Service Agent Robert K. Webster, thirty-seven years old, a one-time forester and landscape architect, was assigned to go from Miami, Florida, to Bimini in the Bahama Islands to investigate a report that quantities of counterfeit twenty- and fifty-dollar bills were being circulated in connection with the sales of whisky to rumrunners.

To travel from Miami to Bimini, arrangements were made for Webster to board Coast Guard Patrol Boat CG-249, commanded by Boatswain Sidney C. Sanderlin. Making up the rest of the crew were:

Victor A. Lamby, Motor Machinist's Mate 1st Class
John A. Robinson, Boatswain's Mate 2nd Class
Hal M. Caudle, Seaman 1st Class

160

Frank Lehman, Motor Machinist's Mate 2nd Class
Lawrence F. Tuten, Boatswain's Mate 1st Class
Jodie L. Hollingsworth, Acting Ship's Cook.

With Agent Webster and the crew aboard, the CG-249 shoved off for Bimini on August 7. At one o'clock that afternoon the Coast Guard Patrol sighted an oncoming vessel which, as it came closer, apparently changed course to avoid a close approach to the Coast Guard boat.

Bo's'n Sanderlin, believing that the other vessel was carrying a load of contraband liquor, headed the CG-249 in the suspect's direction. When it appeared that the suspect did not propose to slow down, Sanderlin grabbed a rifle, fired two or three shots across its bow—and the vessel then hove to.

The CG-249 came alongside and Sanderlin boarded the other vessel, an American Gas Screw V-13997, carrying a crew of two—Horace Alderman and Robert W. Weech, both of Miami. In the bow Sanderlin discovered thirty cases of contraband liquor which the two men had picked up in Bimini and intended to smuggle into Miami.

Sanderlin ordered his crew to transfer the liquor to the CG-249 while he went to the wheelhouse to radio his base for further instructions. Agent Webster helped the Coast Guardsmen to transfer the illicit cargo.

Just as Sanderlin reached the entrance to the wheelhouse the men heard a pistol shot and saw Sanderlin crumple to the deck. A quick glance revealed Alderman holding the gun. The men dashed for cover.

Victor Lamby knew there was a gun in the cabin and started for it. Through the pilothouse he saw Alderman aiming the revolver at him. In an effort to save himself, Lamby leaped to one side, landing on the engine-room hatch, and at that moment Alderman fired. The bullet struck Lamby in the right side and he plunged to the engine room below.

As he fell, the clutch handle of the engine caught in his trouser leg, and when Lamby tried to get loose he discovered that he could not move his legs. The bullet had ripped through his spinal cord and the lower half of his body was completely paralyzed.

Frantically, fearing that the bootlegger would come to the hatch to finish him off, the wounded man ripped his trouser leg until he was free of the clutch handle, then with his hands and arms he dragged himself away from the opening and lay exhausted between the hot engines.

Topside, the rumrunners lined up the Coast Guardsmen and Agent Webster on the deck of the rum boat.

"I got two of you already," Alderman said, "and I'm going to get the rest. There ain't going to be no witnesses, see? If you got any prayers, say 'em, because I'm going to burn your boat and feed all of you to the sharks." He handed the gun to Weech. "Shoot the first man that moves."

Alderman went into the wheelhouse of the Coast Guard vessel and returned quickly with another revolver, evidently taken from Sanderlin's body. He stood on the forward deck and fired the gun into the air, then grinned at the captives. "At least you'll be gettin' killed by your own gun," he said.

The grin vanished and he spoke gruffly to Weech. "Get that liquor back aboard our boat."

Weech transferred the liquor to the rum boat. "Now," Alderman told him, "go below and break the gas line in that patrol boat."

Weech went to the engine room, where he found the wounded Lamby. "Get up, you!" Weech ordered. "Get up and break the gas line on this engine."

"I can't get up," Lamby answered. "I've been shot. I can't move."

Savagely, Weech kicked him in the ribs. "Stop stalling," he said. "Come on, get up!"

"I can't, I can't!" Lamby said. "I tell you I can't move. I'm paralyzed from the waist down."

Weech whacked him on the arm with the barrel of his gun and Lamby cried out with pain. "This is your last chance," Weech said. "If you don't get up and break that gas line I'll kill you."

"Then you'll have to kill me, because I can't move my legs."

The rumrunner stood with his gun aimed at Lamby's head, as though debating whether or not to pull the trigger. Finally he snorted and grabbed a wrench from the wrench board, tearing the gas line loose and twisting it beyond repair. He took a last look at Lamby.

"You'd better get out of here, sailor, or you'll wind up as food for the sharks."

Lamby was already growing faint from his wounds and the heat of the engine room. A few minutes later he was unconscious.

When Weech emerged from the engine room he saw the crew and Webster still held at bay by Alderman aboard the rum boat. Except for Webster and Tuten, they stood on a small raised deck in the stern, but because this deck was not big enough for all of them, Webster and Tuten were in the cockpit.

"Did you break the gas line?" Alderman asked.

"Yeh. And there's a guy down there that's been shot."

"Is he alive?"

"Yeh."

"Then go back and kill him."

Weech scowled. "He's in bad shape. He's prob'ly going to die anyway. I don't like to shoot a wounded man."

Alderman came close to his partner. "You got no guts," he said. "But you better have nerve enough to keep your trap shut about this when we get ashore. You breathe one word about it and I'll blast your head off."

"Don't worry. I'm not that foolish. I'm in it, too, ain't I?"

"Go throw a match into that engine room and let's get this over with."

Tuten, standing next to Webster, spoke up. "If you guys are going to burn the patrol boat you'd better get yours away from it or it'll burn, too."

"Don't you worry, kid," Alderman said, grinning. "I'll take care of that."

Now Webster made a suggestion, fighting for time. "You're being foolish," he told Alderman. "Why kill all of us over such a small load of liquor? You give us the rowboat and put us adrift and you and your partner can take off with the stuff."

"Do I look that stupid?" Alderman asked. "I know your kind, mister. You're one of those guys that's always snooping around for evidence. Well, there ain't going to be no evidence this time, because you and them and it is all going down there." He pointed one finger at the sea.

Weech went to the engine-room hatch of the patrol boat, lighted a match and dropped it in, followed by another. Then he rejoined Alderman.

"Keep an eye on them," Alderman said. "I'm going to start our engine." He went to the engine room of the rum boat and a few moments later the men heard the sputter of the motor. It kept spitting and missing and was obviously not running properly. Alderman returned to the deck and ordered Weech to see if he could fix the engine. Weech gave Alderman his gun and went to the engine room while Alderman sat on the engine-room hatch, his two guns pointed at the prisoners.

After some ten minutes with no sound from the engine Alderman yelled, "What's the matter? Let's get it going!"

Weech yelled something unintelligible.

Another ten minutes went by and there was still no sound of the motor. Alderman, obviously impatient, leaned over to look through the hatch into the engine room. In that split second Agent Webster lunged at the rumrunner, closely followed by Tuten. The others leaped into action.

Alderman pulled the trigger on one gun. Webster uttered a sharp cry and sank to the deck. Tuten grabbed one gun, Hal Caudle the other. Alderman got off two more shots, one of which struck Jodie Hollingsworth and knocked him overboard. The other shot went wild.

John Robinson seized an ice pick lying on the deck of the rum boat and jumped on Alderman, stabbing him four or five times.

"Weech! Weech!" Alderman shouted.

To stop Weech, Hal Caudle grabbed one of the guns and dove into the engine room, where Weech stood with fear in his eyes. Weech fled toward the forward hatch, and Caudle caught up with him as he began to climb up. The Coast Guardsman shoved the gun barrel into Weech's side and pulled the trigger—but the gun did not shoot! Swiftly Caudle yanked back the automatic slide to reload, and pulled the trigger again, but again it failed to fire. Weech now was almost to the deck. Realizing that the gun was empty, Caudle clambered to the deck, grabbed Weech and hit him with the gun butt. John Robinson closed his hands around Weech's throat, then picked him up and hurled him over the side into the sea.

In the water Weech swam to the stern of the patrol boat. There Larry Tuten seized an oar, whacked Weech over the head with it, then reached down and pulled him aboard. Robinson came over with a pair of handcuffs which he snapped on Weech's dripping wrists.

Aboard the rum boat Caudle saw Hollingsworth floundering in the water, bleeding from the wound made by Alderman's shot. He threw him a line and hauled him aboard, where his wound was found to be not critical.

The men tried to help Sanderlin and Webster, but both

were dead. They brought Lamby out of the engine room and made him as comfortable as possible, and in the engine room they found the matches dropped by Weech. Apparently both had gone out before they hit bottom.

John Robinson radioed the Coast Guard base and asked for help. About an hour later Commander Jordan, with an armed force aboard the CG-2246 came alongside, and Commander Jordan took charge.

Victor Lamby, Alderman's second victim, was hospitalized in Miami. He died from his wounds on August 11, four days after the sea battle.

The subsequent investigation of the clash established that it was Agent Webster's attack on Alderman that made it possible for his companions to overpower the rumrunners, who would otherwise surely have carried out their threat to kill them all.

William H. Moran, then Chief of the Secret Service, went to Florida to offer his sympathy to Webster's wife and two children, and to do everything in his power to see that Webster's killer was punished.

On January 26, 1928, at Miami, Florida, Horace Alderman was convicted of murder in the first degree and executed on August 17, 1929.

Robert W. Weech pleaded guilty to a charge of manslaughter at Jacksonville, Florida, on May 31, 1928, and in June was sentenced to serve one year and one day in Atlanta Penitentiary. The court believed that Weech actually had very little to do with the murders, but that he was used as a tool and acted entirely through his own fear of Alderman.

Agent Webster was buried in Arlington National Cemetery, Virginia, and each year the Secret Service sends a delegation of agents from Washington to decorate his grave on Memorial Day.

Killers like Alderman, and potential killers, are found in

all corners of the underworld which is invaded by Treasury law-enforcement agents—the Secret Service, the Bureau of Narcotics, the Bureau of Customs, the Coast Guard, the Alcohol and Tobacco Tax Division—and even by the Intelligence Division of the Internal Revenue Service.

The Intelligence Division is the foe of the tax cheat, and its agents encounter some of the wiliest schemes and schemers ever to try to swindle Uncle Sam.

14

THE TAX DETECTIVES

A messenger from a big trailer-manufacturing company appeared at a teller's window in a bank and laid down several thousand-dollar bills to be deposited in the company's name. Waiting in line directly behind the messenger was an official of the Treasury Department, who chanced to see the transaction and reported it to the Intelligence Division of the Internal Revenue Service.

When Intelligence Division agents investigated the business affairs of the trailer company they discovered that the owners had failed to make records of many sales, had overstated the cost of goods sold and had made a great many fraudulent entries in the company's books.

Result: The four owners were sent to prison for a total of twenty years and were required to pay taxes and penalties amounting to $1,150,786.08.

Although the vast majority of our taxpayers are honest, the agents of the Intelligence Division have found that tax dodgers include funeral directors, schoolteachers, stevedores, farmers, electricians—practically every job category from actors to zoologists—you name the occupation and the Intelligence Division will have worked it.

Tax evasion is another form of smuggling and, like Customs agents, the agents of the Intelligence Division have vigilant eyes. One collegiate joker has suggested as their theme song, *The Eyes of Taxes* "are upon you all the livelong day; the eyes of taxes are upon you, you cannot get away. . . ." And those eyes see the small-time—as well as the big-time—tax cheats who hide their money and fake their tax forms and mistakenly believe the government will never find them out.

The principal income of our federal government, before the enactment of the Sixteenth Amendment to the Constitution on February 25, 1913, was from Customs duties and excise or indirect taxes.

Under the Sixteenth Amendment the first income tax was enacted by Congress on October 3, 1913, and is known as the Revenue Act of 1913. It imposed a tax of one per cent on net incomes of individuals, estates, trusts and corporations. A surtax, or extra tax, graduated from one to six per cent, was applied to incomes exceeding twenty thousand dollars.

In 1916 another law doubled the rates specified in the 1913 act, to provide for increased government costs, and the surtax rates were raised, running from one per cent on incomes of twenty thousand dollars to thirteen per cent on incomes of two million dollars or more.

When the United States entered World War I on April 6, 1917, it soon became evident that this country would have to help its European allies financially, so the income tax rates were again increased and an excess-profits tax was also imposed.

To perform the growing paper work, more and more people were hired by the Bureau of Internal Revenue (the official name today is the Internal Revenue Service). On June 30, 1913, the bureau had about four thousand employees. On June 30, 1919, this number had grown to more than fourteen thousand. In 1959 it was about fifty thousand.

In 1919 many serious complaints reached the then Commissioner of Internal Revenue Daniel C. Roper (later Secretary of Commerce) concerning alleged tax frauds and dishonest employees. Commissioner Roper had previously served as First Assistant Postmaster General and had become familiar with the work of the Post Office inspectors, whose job it was to investigate frauds in the use of the mails and dishonesty among Post Office workers. The Commissioner decided to create an Intelligence Division to make similar investigations in the Bureau of Internal Revenue.

On July 1, 1919, with the approval of the Secretary of the Treasury and the Postmaster General, six Post Office inspectors were transferred to the Bureau of Internal Revenue. One of these, Mr. Elmer L. Irey, was chosen to head the new unit, and he became a famous figure in American law enforcement when his agents later sent to prison more formidable gangsters, racketeers and other notorious criminals than any other enforcement organization. In fact, the man credited with gathering the evidence that convicted Al Capone, overlord of the Chicago underworld, was Frank J. Wilson, a special agent of the Intelligence Division, who later became Chief of the United States Secret Service.

One of the most important investigations in which the Intelligence Division took part had no direct relation to tax evasion matters. This was the famous Lindbergh kidnaping case, in which the young son of Colonel Charles Lindbergh, world-famous flier, was taken from his bedroom and later found dead.

On March 8, 1932, Colonel Lindbergh telephoned the

Secretary of the Treasury and asked if the Intelligence Division might assist in bringing about the return of his son, who was apparently being held for ransom.

In conference with Colonel Lindbergh and his attorney, Mr. Irey and his special agents discussed plans for the payment of the ransom money to the kidnaper. The Colonel and others were anxious to deliver the payment, but the Intelligence Division agents insisted upon making a written record of the serial number of each ransom bill. Also, they insisted upon including thirty-five thousand dollars in gold certificates in the ransom cash. (Gold certificates were taken out of circulation in 1933.)

Contacts were made with the kidnaper and the money was delivered, but later developments proved that the Lindbergh child had been dead before the negotiations were begun.

The identity of the kidnaper was unknown until some two years after the crime. On September 12, 1934, an attendant in a gasoline station in New York City noticed a ten-dollar gold certificate which was handed to him by a customer in payment for gasoline. The attendant had not seen a gold certificate in some time, and on the chance that it might be a counterfeit, he wrote the license number of the customer's car on the bill, which was later deposited in a New York bank.

A bank clerk checked the serial number of the gold certificate with the list of numbers of the Lindbergh ransom currency furnished to banks by the Intelligence Division. It proved to be one of the ransom bills, and the license number led straight to the home of Bruno Richard Hauptmann, a German carpenter, who was arrested, convicted and executed for the kidnaping.

Later Colonel Lindbergh expressed his appreciation to Mr. Irey. "If it had not been for your service being in the case," the Colonel said, "Hauptmann would not now be on trial and your organization deserves the full credit for his apprehension."

Agents of the Intelligence Division are experts at locating hidden evidence and are skilled in methods of figuring the true income of an individual or a corporation who seeks to hide it by manipulating records. Some of their investigations are based upon information received from discharged or disgruntled employees, from lovelorn and neglected secretaries, suspicious partners, or even close friends who pay their just taxes and who resent the fact that others are trying to cheat Uncle Sam.

Some of the investigations begin with informants who are seeking rewards. The Intelligence Division is authorized to pay not more than ten per cent of money recovered in taxes, penalties and fines, depending upon the amount of assistance and co-operation given by the informant. If you reported to the Intelligence Division that your neighbor must be evading taxes because "he lives like a king," the chances are that you would receive very little in reward money if your suspicions were correct, because the Intelligence Division agents would have to make a complete investigation. If, however, you were a bookkeeper for a firm and reported that your employer was keeping two sets of books in order to evade payment of taxes, you might be in a position to get photostatic copies of books and reports for the Intelligence Division. In that even, if your employer was convicted as a tax evader, and if the money recovered, including taxes, penalties and fines, should total two hundred and fifty thousand dollars, you would undoubtedly receive a full ten per cent payment of twenty-five thousand dollars.

Sometimes tax dodgers are exposed when they receive money from some source which reports the payment when the tax dodgers don't report it. One disc jockey in Philadelphia was fined twenty-five hundred dollars for evading payment of six thousand dollars in income taxes from 1949 to 1954. In this case the disc jockey found that "payola" doesn't pay. Payola is the payment of money "under the table" by phonograph record distributors to disc jockeys, in order to induce them to plug certain records on the air. The Philadelphia broadcaster had failed to report payola income of more than twenty-two thousand dollars in six years. His trouble was that the recording companies who made the payolas reported them on their tax returns.

One seagoing investigation revealed that several fishing boat captains and crew members were evading taxes. The crew members refused to work unless their skippers consented to understate the amount of their earnings. They were convicted.

In Florida, a filling station operator ran an illegal lottery, reporting his filling station income but not his gambling earnings. High living betrayed his wealth and a jury refused to believe his story that he had dug up a fortune in long-buried savings.

Phony tax experts also underestimate the ability of the tax detectives. One convicted "expert" falsified seven tax returns for clients, but signed his name in disappearing ink so that when the fraud was discovered his name had vanished—until it was scientifically restored by the Treasury agents.

Most common techniques of tax evasion are (1) the omission and understatement of income, (2) padding expenses with mythical or unallowable items, and (3) the falsification of credits, especially those for personal and family exemptions. The tax cheat generally spends his "loot" on himself or his family. A new house, new car, lavish entertaining, may betray his fraud. Most tax dodgers think they can successfully conceal cash, but the entire banking system of the country co-operates with the Treasury by making systematic reports of unusual currency transactions. Many are legitimate, but some furnish leads to schemers who greedily shirk their responsibilities as taxpayers only to wind up as defendants in a federal courtroom.

One fabulous tax hider was secretary of a steel-casting company and tossed money around like falling leaves. A worthy host, he made a specialty of duck dinners with oranges stuffed in the mouths of the roasted birds. Gifts of liquor included in shipments of castings "helped maintain good will," he said. Salaries for servants and personal expenses were paid by his company "because increased work resulted in some bookkeeping mistakes." Horse racing was one of his weaknesses and when money was rolling in he laid bets on horses all over the country. On one race his winnings were fifty thousand dollars, and twenty-thousand-dollar afternoons were frequent. He demanded payment in cash, but always paid his losses by check. Soon he established his own stables with a string of eighteen race horses.

Suddenly his luck changed. He plunged heavily. Bookmakers refused to take his bets. Finally agents of the Intelligence Division checked his company's books and uncovered all the tricks—pay roll padding, phony purchases, false expense accounts, bonuses to employees, who had to "kick back," and black market deals. Result: The taxpayer was found guilty of a one-million-five-hundred-thousand-dollar income tax fraud and was sentenced to serve five years in jail. Among other things, the investigation disclosed that his future, as predicted in the 1912 Class Prophecy at his high school graduation, was a little off center. The class had voted him the "most likely to succeed as a preacher and famous author."

Another case demonstrates the close tie between the Intelligence Division and the ATTD. A dapper Cincinnati whisky broker formed a syndicate in 1942 and cornered one hundred thousand barrels of whisky, knowing that wartime shortages would send prices skyrocketing. He and his associates made some two million dollars in over-ceiling cash payments. One dealer testified that he paid more than two hundred thousand dollars for deliveries of whisky, brandy and rum. Single payments in cash ranged as high as forty thousand dollars. ATTD agents brought the dealer to trial, reported his illicit riches to the Intelligence Division. He was sentenced to six years in prison and fined two hundred and forty thousand dollars, and another fine of two hundred and forty thousand dollars was slapped on his company.

The widespread practice of offering tips and gratuities for services and special favors often reaches the proportion of big business, and even the cash customers of the popular dining and entertainment places in our larger cities may be surprised at the sums involved in just one tax investigation made by the Intelligence Division.

The agents discovered that in a seven-year period the former headwaiter of the banquet department of a large New York City hotel received more than two hundred thousand dollars in tips! Unfortunately for him, he reported only sixty-six thousand dollars of this for income tax purposes. Additional taxes and penalties assessed were ninety-six thousand dollars, and the offender was sentenced to four months in prison and fined seventy-five hundred dollars. The agents were aided in their investigation by the fact that the hotel added a flat fifteen per cent to the price of food and beverages sold to their banquet clients, for distribution as tips to the service personnel, and records were kept of these currency transactions.

One man living in Truth or Consequences, New Mexico, tried his hand at altering W-2 forms, which show the amount of tax withheld by an employer from each employee. The Truth or Consequences man placed the figure "1" in front of the amount of tax withheld, and each year for four years he received a refund of one hundred dollars or more to which he was not entitled. The Intelligence Division checked his income tax returns and questioned him about the insertion of the numeral. He told the truth, but had to take the consequences—he was sentenced to prison for one year and one day.

In another city a man who owned four theaters tried to evade taxes on admissions and income by placing extra unrecorded rolls of tickets on sale at certain times. Money from the sale of these extra tickets was never reported. On his pay roll he placed the names of six purely fictitious people and showed that he paid each of them fifty dollars a week. Two assistants who worked for the owner were paid eight thousand dollars a year, and although they reported this amount on their income tax returns they actually kept only fifty-two hundred dollars and "kicked back" twenty-eight hundred dollars to the owner, who failed to report it in his income. His scheme was soon uncovered by the agents and he was sentenced and fined.

One tax fraud case began when an alert operator of an office machine in the office of the Collector of Internal Revenue noticed that within a short time she had typed slips for four income tax refunds to be mailed to the same address in Hollywood, California. Since it was possible that government checks were being—or had been—forged by this taxpayer, the Intelligence Division asked the Secret Service to join in the investigation, along with the Post Office inspectors.

The agents descended upon the office of a special accountant and real estate broker in Hollywood, where they were able to prove that he had filed fictitious income tax returns, claimed fraudulent refunds, forged an endorsement on a government refund check and had used the mails to defraud. Actually he filed thirty-eight false income tax returns in twelve different collection districts. He was sentenced to one year and one day in prison and to pay a fine of three thousand dollars.

On November 1, 1951, the Internal Revenue Service was charged with the enforcement of federal laws relating to gambling, and agents of the Intelligence Division, like those in the other Treasury enforcement agencies, often do undercover work in dealing with gamblers who are large-scale tax cheats. One agent posed as a soldier on leave, frequented suspected gambling houses and developed enough leads and evidence for other agents to crack down on a city-wide bookmaking operation.

Agents dressed as laborers have watched and recorded big gambling pay-offs, identifying operators and players, and in some cases actually making plays for evidence. One agent, working under cover, was called upon to hold a flashlight while a mechanic repaired the inner workings of a slot machine!

In 1956 a squad of thirty-five Intelligence Division agents, working with twenty plain-clothes detectives of the New York City Police Department, prepared to squash a multimillion-dollar numbers racket. The agents and detectives, wearing windbreakers and work clothes, stationed themselves in the neighborhood. Some in automobiles kept in contact by short-wave radio to co-ordinate the forthcoming raids.

Early in the afternoon two policewomen, wearing civilian clothes appropriate for the neighborhood, were sent to a nineteen-apartment gray brick building. They had with them a jar of Vaseline mixed with phosphorescent powder. As they entered the apartment house, one of them smeared a dab of this concoction on the doorknob of the outside door to the apartment house.

A short while later a known suspect was seen entering the building. Within a few moments the agents and detectives rushed into the building and checked the doorknobs of each apartment with a portable ultra-violet light. At apartment 3-A, invisible to the naked eye but glowing under the special rays, was the tell-tale phosphorescence. They broke down the door and found the nineteen operators and headquarters of the gambling ring. The evidence included more than one million policy slips representing about seventy-five thousand to one hundred thousand dollars—the "take" for one day's policy operation.

Other raids were made on the West Side and throughout the Harlem area, netting thirty-eight alleged "bankers" and "runners."

What about the taxing of the lucky contestants who win large sums of money or fabulous quantities of merchandise on radio and television quiz programs? Says Clifford W. Stowe, Assistant Commissioner of Internal Revenue, "We deal with the winners of large sums of money on so-called giveaway programs just as we do with people who are in short-life professions. We devote the same attention to those people who get what you might call a windfall type of income as we do with a person who receives his income in large purses but over a very short period of time. The basic problem insofar as winners of TV programs are concerned is the same as that we have with respect to prize fighters, actors and people in similar activities."

The only difference between these people and the average taxpayer is that the Internal Revenue Service makes it a point to check the next quarterly returns of the big-money winners to make sure their windfalls are properly reported.

In these instances the Internal Revenue Service has access to the records of the broadcasting companies, knows exactly what prizes are awarded and the values of the prizes. Moreover, the broadcasting companies must report all payments they make, so that any contestant who wilfully fails to declare his winnings as income must expect to reckon with the tax detectives and to face the possibility of being fined and imprisoned.

There are still some people who profess ignorance of Uncle Sam's tax programs and policies. A midwestern farmer, for instance, did not file income tax returns for several years, and an Intelligence Division agent called on him to find out why. The farmer claimed ignorance of the tax laws, seemed surprised to learn that he was supposed to have executed tax forms, and listened patiently while the agent made a long and detailed explanation about income taxes. When the investigator finished, the farmer scratched his head and said, "Well, young fella, I guess you got a purty good thing there, all right—but I don't think I want to join. Some other time, maybe."

P.S. He joined.

We have explored the kinds of cases which the Treasury agent investigates—cases that send the chill of fear up his spine (for he is only human), cases that bring compassion to his heart, weariness to his body and occasionally laughter to his soul.

Now we will take a closer look at the kinds of men who are chosen to do this work, and at the qualifications one must have if he is interested in becoming a Treasury enforcement agent.

15

HOW TO BECOME
A TREASURY AGENT

The men who work as Treasury agents come from all
parts of the country and from many walks of life. In the
Secret Service alone you could once find a former circus
promotion man, a private detective, insurance detective,
state police officer, newspaper reporter, court stenographer,
professional baseball player, lawyer, accountant, statisti-
cian—even an undertaker!

Years ago a youth who worked as a bootblack in Pennsylvania was recruited to help Secret Service men trap a
counterfeiting gang. As a result of this exciting adventure,
the youngster became anxious to join the Secret Service and
he finally did. After several years he was offered—and he
accepted—an attractive job with the Hearst newspapers.
Subsequently he became the confidential assistant to President Herbert Hoover, a post which Mr. Lawrence Richey,
the former Secret Service man, still holds as this is written.

While some other Treasury agents have voluntarily
ended their government careers to accept attractive offers
from American industry, most of them find the law-en-

forcement profession rewarding enough, exciting enough and sufficiently attractive, in general, to stick with it as a lifetime occupation.

Each of these men must be intelligent, observant, tactful and courageous. He must have the education, confidence and poise needed to confer with public officials, bank presidents, merchants, scholars and people in all other occupations and professions. He must also have the ability to fit himself naturally into any situation or emergency, adjusting to each new environment like a human chameleon.

He must be fair and impartial in his investigations, and constantly aware that his job is to get facts so justice may be done. Personal prejudices or unsupported opinions have no place in his work.

He must be prepared to travel on short notice, to move his family from one part of the country to another, if so ordered, and to work for long periods without rest when necessary, conscious of the fact that criminals do not keep office hours.

He is expected to keep his own counsel and not to discuss his work with outsiders.

He should be able to express himself clearly in writing, for he must prepare intelligible reports for his superiors and make detailed reports to federal prosecutors in cases to be tried in court; he may often enter into correspondence to seek information from various individuals or firms.

Above all, his personal conduct and deportment must be absolutely above reproach.

So far as salary is concerned it isn't the highest-paying job in the world, but the pay is much better than in many other fields, ranging upward from about five thousand dollars a year. A Treasury agent gets liberal vacations and sick leave and is eligible to retire at the minimum age of fifty years, with a minimum of twenty years' service. He can buy life insurance at extremely low costs, and if he retires he may retain the insurance cost-free until he is sixty-five years old. At that time the amount of the insurance policy decreases gradually until it reaches twenty-five per cent of the original total, and there it remains until the insured dies, when it is paid to his beneficiaries.

These are some of the advantages that make the job of the Treasury agent attractive. As in other fields, there are also disadvantages. The agent may be called upon to work at very irregular hours, to take personal risks, to be exposed to all kinds of weather, to engage in arduous physical exertion, to work in strange and often distasteful environments and to travel considerably.

Treasury agents are appointed under rules of the United States Civil Service Commission. The men selected for these jobs must be able to recognize and develop evidence, to testify in court and to meet the other qualifications we have mentioned.

The nature and extent of a Treasury agent's duties have been described in the actual cases already recited.

The man who wants to be a Treasury agent (women are not eligible for such appointments, but are employed as clerks and stenographers) should have a college degree, preferably with college training in police administration, police science, criminology, law or law enforcement. Some colleges which offer such courses are:

> Indiana University, Bloomington, Indiana.
> Los Angeles City College, Los Angeles, California.
> Michigan State College, East Lansing, Michigan.
> Northwestern University, Chicago, Illinois.
> San Jose State College, San Jose, California.
> State College of Washington, Pullman, Washington.
> University of Southern California, Los Angeles,
>   California.
> University of Wichita, Wichita, Kansas.

Every appointment to the Treasury enforcement agencies is made subject to a satisfactory investigation. Each candidate is investigated thoroughly to secure evidence of his loyalty to the United States, his honesty, integrity and general character. Evidence of his habitual use of intoxicants, any disloyalty, immorality, disrespect for law, unethical dealings or material misstatements of facts on his application forms, will be grounds for his rejection. By the time the Treasury finishes its character investigation of a would-be Treasury enforcement agent, it knows more about the man than he knows about himself.

If you want more information about qualifications, or about Civil Service examinations for a job as Treasury enforcement agent, you should address a letter to (or call on) the Treasury Board of United States Civil Service Examiners in or nearest to the city where you live. A list of locations of these Examiners' Boards will be found in the back of this book. Tell the board what you want to know, and be specific about the kind of job you have in mind.

If you aim at a federal law-enforcement career, you can do no better than to try for an appointment as a Treasury agent. And please notice that we haven't used the term "T-Man" at any other place in this book. "T-Man" is a catch phrase that may have been coined by some detective story writer and obviously suggested by the designation "G-Man," which was applied to FBI agents. Both "G-Man" and "T-Man" are occasionally heard in the argot of the underworld, but in respectable society and among his fellows the Treasury man prefers to be identified with the agency for which he works; he wants to be known as a Secret Service agent, a Customs agent, a Narcotic agent, and so on.

This is quite understandable. When a man devotes his energy, his skills, his time, and willingly risks his very life to enforce certain laws of our United States, then it is obvious that he undertakes this task with a great deal of personal pride. This, perhaps, is the real secret of the success of the Treasury enforcement agencies—the pride of the men in their work and in their respective branches of service.

Sometimes the agents seem disgruntled; they complain about long hours; they gripe about unpleasant assignments and about other matters, real or imagined—but in the long run they enjoy what they do. Individually they are Treasury agents, and proud of it. Collectively they are the Secret Service, the Bureau of Narcotics, the Bureau of Customs, the Intelligence Division, the Alcohol and Tobacco Tax Division, the United States Coast Guard. They are the Treasury enforcement agencies—six against the underworld —the most efficient group of law men in action today.

BIBLIOGRAPHY

Counterfeiting—Crime Against the People, by Laurence Dwight Smith. W. W. Norton, New York, 1944.

Customs Hints. Pamphlet, Bureau of Customs, Treasury Department, Washington 25, D.C.

Know Your Money. Booklet, U.S. Secret Service, Treasury Department, Washington 25, D.C.

Living Death—The Truth About Drug Addiction. Pamphlet, Bureau of Narcotics, Treasury Department, Washington 25, D.C.

Machine Guns and Certain Other Firearms. Booklet. Internal Revenue Service, Treasury Department, Washington 25, D.C.

Men Against Crime, by John J. Floherty. Lippincott, New York, 1946.

Reilly of the White House, by Michael F. Reilly. Simon & Schuster, New York, 1947.

Starling of the White House, by Edmund W. Starling. Simon & Schuster, New York, 1946.

Story of the Secret Service, The, by Ferdinand Kuhn. Random House, New York, 1957.

Treasury Agent—The Inside Story, by Andrew J. Tully. Simon & Schuster, New York, 1958.

Uncle Sam's Treasury, by Robert Disraeli. Little, Brown & Co., Boston, 1941.

United States Secret Service—What It Is—What It Does. Booklet, U.S. Secret Service, Treasury Department, Washington 25, D.C.

United States Treasury, The. Booklet, Treasury Information Service, Treasury Department, Washington 25, D.C.

SOURCES OF FURTHER INFORMATION

Bureau of Customs,
Treasury Department,
Washington 25, D.C.

Bureau of Narcotics,
Treasury Department,
1300 E Street, N. W.,
Washington 25, D.C.

Intelligence Division,
Internal Revenue Service,
Treasury Department,
Washington 25, D.C.

Alcohol and Tobacco Tax Division,
Internal Revenue Service,
Treasury Department,
Washington 25, D.C.

U.S. Coast Guard,
Treasury Department,
1300 E Street, N. W.,
Washington 25, D.C.

U.S. Secret Service,
Treasury Department,
Washington 25, D.C.

U.S. Civil Service Commission,
Washington 25, D.C.

TREASURY BOARDS OF UNITED STATES CIVIL SERVICE EXAMINERS

Atlanta
(Alabama, Canal Zone, Florida,
Georgia, Mississippi, North
Carolina, South Carolina, Tennessee)
827 Peachtree-Seventh Building,
50 Seventh Street, N. E.,
Atlanta 5, Georgia.

Boston
(Connecticut, Maine, Massachusetts,
New Hampshire, Rhode Island, Vermont)
55 Tremont Street,
Boston 8, Massachusetts.

Chicago
(Illinois, Michigan, Wisconsin)
17 North Dearborn Street,
Chicago 2, Illinois.

Cincinnati
(Indiana, Kentucky, Ohio, Virginia,
West Virginia)
Post Office Building, Box 2119,
Cincinnati 1, Ohio.

Dallas
(Arkansas, Louisiana, New Mexico,
Oklahoma, Texas)
1114 Commerce Street,
Dallas 2, Texas.

New York
   (New York, Puerto Rico, Virgin Islands)
   90 Church Street,
   New York 7, New York.

Omaha
   (Colorado, Iowa, Kansas, Minnesota,
   Missouri, Nebraska, North Dakota,
   South Dakota, Wyoming)
   100 Elks Club Building,
   Omaha 2, Nebraska.

Philadelphia
   (Delaware, District of Columbia,
   Maryland, New Jersey, Pennsylvania)
   1700 Widener Building,
   Philadelphia 7, Pennsylvania.

San Francisco
   (Alaska, Arizona, California,
   Hawaii, Idaho, Montana, Nevada,
   Oregon, Utah, Washington)
   715 Flood Building,
   870 Market Street,
   San Francisco 2, California.

INDEX